KICKING
OUT THE
Bucket List

A Wood Dragon Book

ADVANCE PRAISE FOR KICKING OUT THE BUCKET LIST

This book is perfect for adventurous people or those who love to read about personal experiences in new places. There is so much detail and emotion in Glenda's descriptions of what she has experienced that I feel that I have a personal tour guide to behind the scenes. I also appreciated the little tips she gave during her "Done & Dusted" that would certainly be helpful if I was to travel to that location or on that adventure. The "Points for Reflection" throughout the book made me reflect on my own activities and adventures—and not just about the adventures, but about the experience itself. For example, one reflection point was: "Think about those things you have completed or achieved through pure grit ..." I loved that. Although I'm not a traveller, I enjoyed reading about the depth of Glenda's experiences. I NOW may consider doing more virtual tours of some of these places.

Lisa Peters, TV & Podcast Host, Community Developer

Kicking Out the Bucket List is perfect for people who, like me, like to reflect on life but have read too many books where the author inflicts their wisdom on the reader. This book is perfect for someone who wants to enjoy having a window into someone else's thinking, but also wants to independently interpret ideas and then reflect on their significance. Through the reflection process highlighted in the book, I learned that what I have achieved or experienced came from seizing the moment rather than having a lifelong plan or goal. I also learned that reflection on the past can uncover patterns and priorities in a more enjoyable way than trying to plan for the future when there is finite time but infinite options. The trust the author showed in sharing personal details pulled me into the book and then kept me interested; I felt like I was sitting at a campfire enjoying a cup of soup while also being able to participate in the conversation by reflecting on my own experiences. I would recommend this book to people who are interested in authentic, vulnerable storytelling from an author who clearly presents her own experience and leaves the reader to form their own views. I would also recommend the book to anyone who would like to ponder the value and opportunities of their life with gratitude and honesty, rather than trying to adopt someone else's formula for success.

James King, Author of KingsInsight, Agile Coach

Kicking Out the Bucket List is a great book for anyone reassessing their life goals. It has numerous stories that provide examples to others about what you can do if you are able, fit and willing. An easy-to-read book—you can just pick it up and read a chapter or two in any order—then think and ponder.

Marcella Lazarus, Executive Coach, Director

The book highlights the power of taking opportunities as they arise, of being open to new, unknown, unthought about, unplanned adventures. To be aware of your fears, what they are telling you, and then to move through them and enjoy the experience of the adventure! Get on with it! For you never know the impact you can have on others that will lift them, encourage them, or stir their passion and motivation! This book made me realize that life is far from over, that I have lots left to live and give and experience. Although my body doesn't always want to play ball, there is much that I can celebrate, embrace and be grateful for having done and achieved in my life. This book served as a wake-up call to be more celebratory for what I have done, including the things that aren't necessarily in congruency with what society thinks are important, but are significant to me. It encouraged me to be more intentional about the adventures I want to live and still experience, and to be more open and aware of opportunities. This book is a must read for everyone who wants to experience the fullness of life and the adventures that await. It is an opportunity to reflect and step out to truly live!

Peter Ainley, CEO & Founder, LOS Global,
Executive Leadership Strategies

This book is not only a great adventure book, but also material to use during self-reflection. The many questions throughout the book make you marvel about the life you've lived and the precious moments you haven't thought about for a time. With its stories and questions for reflection, this book helped to keep my spark of adventure alive. I will read it again, probably multiple times, and use it as a reference for recording my future adventures so I don't fall into the trap of always wishing for the next best thing in order to be fulfilled and content.

Travis Robbins, US Marine, Founder Pains to Profits

KICKING
OUT THE
Bucket List

LIVING LIFE
WITH INTENTION
AND PASSION

by
GLENDA MITCHELL

A Wood Dragon Book

Published by:
Wood Dragon Books
Box 429, Mossbank, Saskatchewan, Canada, S0H 3G0
http://www.wooddragonbooks.com

Cover design: Callum Jagger, Hyperlight Artwork
Interior design: Christine Lee

ISBN: 978-1-990863-62-2 (eBook)
ISBN: 978-1-990863-61-5 (Hardcover)
ISBN: 978-1-990863-60-8 (Paperback)

To contact the author:
Website: https://mitchell.news/
Email: kickingoutthebucketlist@mitchell.news

In loving memory of

my father, whose determination and quest
for excellence lives on in these pages

Dedicated to

my mother, whose ongoing desire to grow and
learn has inspired me to reach for the stars

TABLE OF CONTENTS

1

Quest for Success

Spent on the outskirts of a relatively small town in South Africa with my mother, father, and two older brothers, my early years could be considered idyllic. My dad was a successful businessman, and my mother was dedicated to her family. She has always lived with the attitude that the day you stop learning and trying new things is the day you die. Passionate about making the most of every day that she has been given, she encouraged me to do the same.

I was a confident young girl, feeling the need to do everything that everyone else did and to be the best at it. Every time someone told me what they had done, I wanted to do it too. Additionally, if I did do it, it was typically not enough to just enjoy the experience—I was determined to win. I had to be faster, climb higher, or score more. Often I did. When I failed to do so, I usually came close.

My older brothers saw themselves as protectors of their little sister, but I saw them as my competition. I had to chase them, keep up with them, beat them.

Not only were my brothers my competition, but so were my classmates. Even though I was always the youngest in the class at primary school, I excelled in everything I tried. I was captain of the netball team, on top of the tennis ladder, first in class, winner of multiple subject awards, and played the lead in the school plays. Although not quite at the top, I still fared well on the swimming team and made it into the school choir. From the age of five, I won gold medals in dancing eisteddfods and passed my ballet, tap, and modern dance exams with distinction.

What seemed to be the first real curve ball in my almost-perfect life came when I was told that I was leaving the town of my formative years and moving to a tiny town that I had never heard of. I was to leave my friends and everything I knew. I even had to go to boarding school! Despite my homesickness and moving to a new school in the middle of the school year, I managed to become involved in numerous activities and shine. Most sports came to me easily and I was at or near the top of the class academically. As a school choir member and leader of the music band, I was part of numerous community performances. The debating team liked having me on their side, the art teacher was sad when I stopped going to the craft club, and the tennis coach used to grapple with my dance teacher for my attention.

Leaving school and entering university was the first time I experienced material doubts about my own ability. It was the first time I can remember wondering whether I was able to do something. Prior to that, I had simply assumed I could do anything that I tried—and do so at a high level. I had never needed to motivate myself by saying, "I can" as I had never considered there was another possibility. But at university, I was thrown into a big pool with a large number of fish, and whilst I did not sink, I did not swim too well either.

There were many good things that arose from my university years—not least of all meeting my husband Walter—but there were also a number of disappointments. Although I had experienced challenges in the past, I was unable to remember experiencing many major setbacks and so I had limited knowledge of how to deal with those situations when they occurred. Most of all, I did not know how to deal with not winning, not being at the top, not being the best. I started having doubts about my ability to be successful.

Once I completed my degree and entered the workforce, I advanced quickly into advisory roles, sitting alongside corporate executives in board meetings. I still felt the need to be better than others in order to succeed.

With my brother having moved across the seas, Walter and I decided to do the same. We were young, held the right qualifications to be accepted by Australia and were up for an adventure. If I thought that going to university had taken me out of my comfort zone, moving countries was on an entirely different level. This time, I felt as though I was a tiny fish in a big ocean.

My desire to be successful in my chosen country led me to continue my business career trajectory. I also competed in running events, played netball, and performed in various dance groups. I travelled extensively and took on as many adventurous pursuits as I could. Although I was fortunate to have done so many things and excelled at many of them, I struggled to be satisfied. It was as if I was creating this never-ending list of achievements to tick off. Each time I felt as though I was reaching the finishing posts, I moved them. I was measuring my satisfaction against a moving target.

2

A Pivotal Moment

In 2016, I found myself in hospital with a 36 cm blood clot in my right leg (Deep Vein Thrombosis – or DVT) and multiple clots in my lungs (Pulmonary Emboli or PE). Based on that statement alone, I can understand if you make the assumption that I ate badly, was obese, had diabetes, was lazy—or all of the above. Even if these assumptions were true, the DVT would have been a shock. I felt as though I was in the prime of my life. I had completed a marathon a couple of months before and considered myself one of the fittest and healthiest people I knew. Friends and family believed the same. I was dumbfounded.

I intentionally stayed away from Dr Google, relying on the "in the flesh" doctors to be the experts. The internet is full of good content, but it can be difficult to discern which pieces of the often-conflicting information are true. In spite of my competitive nature, I do recognise that I cannot be an authority on all topics and have a tendency to trust experts. I did not want to create unnecessary panic in myself or others, so allowed the medical information to be processed step by step, and dealt with challenges as they arose.

In my naivety, I was stunned when a few days after I left the hospital, a well-meaning friend said, "You could have died." I have since found out that PE is one of the most common heart and blood vessel diseases in the world and is associated with a significant mortality rate. I was astonished to discover that one third of people with a pulmonary embolism die before they receive a diagnosis and treatment.

Whilst sore and uncomfortable, a blood clot in the deep venous system of the leg in itself is not particularly dangerous. It becomes life-threatening when a piece of the blood clot breaks off, travels through the circulation system to the heart, enters one of the pulmonary arteries and becomes lodged, creating a pulmonary embolism. The pulmonary arteries transport blood from the right side of the heart to the lungs where the blood carries oxygen and other nutrients to the cells. The heart is the muscle pump that drives the blood through the body. In short, a PE can impact the core body functions. I could have had a heart attack or a stroke.

In the decades leading up to my DVT/PE episode, I had experienced numerous significant changes in my life. I had moved schools, towns, and even countries. I had lost my maternal and paternal grandparents and had experienced the death of my dear, loving dad. I had married. These things all affected the trajectory of my life and contributed to building my character. But for some reason, this near-death experience was my greatest single life-changing moment. I am not scared of death, but for a while, I was worried that I did not have as much life left in me as I had assumed. Maybe I did not have sufficient years left to do what I wanted to do, what I thought I should do, or what I believed others expected me to accomplish. What if I did not have the chance to do it all? I felt as though I had aged twenty years overnight!

My reaction was to start "measuring my life."

3

Measuring Life

I needed a measure to judge whether what I had done was enough.

Ever since the 2007 movie of the same name, *the bucket list* has become a popular life-planning tool. Measuring against a *bucket list* is now a common method of gauging a person's success or worth. It is employed to list those things someone feels **they should do** in their life. It is also used to assess whether someone has done everything **they should have done** in their life.

In the movie *The Bucket List*, two elderly men—blue-collar automotive mechanic Carter Chambers and billionaire Edward Cole—meet for the first time while both are patients in a private hospital that is owned by Edward.

Carter, a gifted amateur historian and family man, wanted to become a history professor in his youth but chose to start a family instead. Edward, a four-time divorced healthcare tycoon and cultured loner, enjoys drinking kopi luwak (one of the most expensive coffees in the world) and relishes mocking his personal valet. The only thing they have in common is the fact that they have both been diagnosed with terminal lung cancer.

While in the hospital, Carter and Edward manage to find common ground. For fun, Carter starts writing a list of activities to do before he "kicks the bucket." After hearing he has less than a year to live, he dejectedly discards his list, feeling as though he is already out of time. Edward finds the list and urges him to do everything on it, adding his own items and offering to finance all expenses. Carter agrees and the two patients begin their globetrotting adventures.

There is little or no known evidence that a *bucket list* was used as a "list of things to do before you die" before the movie. It is believed that Justin Zackham, the writer of the screenplay, coined the expression "*bucket list*" after he wrote his own "List of Things to Do Before I Kick the Bucket" and shortened it to "Justin's *Bucket List*". The first item on his list was to "get a film made at a major studio." This list gave him the idea for the screenplay and *The Bucket List* became his first studio film.

It is amazing how quickly the term has become commonplace. Even more so, it is astounding how many people seem to have started living or measuring their lives according to a list of things they or others think they should do. Increasingly, the measurement of self-worth appears to focus on ticking off adventurous pursuits completed and global destinations reached, as emphasised by the characters in the movie.

As a poignant example of this, in 2022, I came across two billboards in the small coastal town of Airlie Beach, Australia, each advertising adventures; one challenging people with "Before I die ..." and the other listing activities and prices for "*Bucket List* Items" in the area. Nearly every week, I come across newspaper reports, travel blogs, or motivational articles referring to the *bucket list*. These write-ups either promote a list of things someone should do before they die or detail what one or more persons have done or plan to do because they are worried about not doing it before they run out of time.

I frequently have people tell me that they have added something new to their *bucket list*. Sometimes the item is inspired by one of my stories. Although I am glad that one of my stories has inspired others, I have come to observe that in many cases the item never gets beyond being an item on a list. In some cases, the inaction is due to a lack of time or money. But in many cases, the inaction is due to limited importance being placed on completing the item. People add items to their *bucket list* because they have heard about others who have added the same item to their list. It sounds exciting at the time, but in the end, they assign limited value to the item, which in turn decreases motivation and interest.

There are many articles on how to build a *bucket list*. Look online and you will find spreadsheets, tables, books, blogs, websites, and apps to help create your life "to-do" list. What there is not as much of is how to make the most out of life, to maximise the value of personal gifts and strengths. Maybe that is why there are so many people with more things on their *bucket list* than they will ever have the time to complete. The list grows and soon the positive feelings that accompanied the addition of an item disappear; the fun things on the list pile up and somehow they do not seem to feel like so much fun anymore. The *bucket list* controls the person rather than being a source of motivation or inspiration. A source of angst rather than jubilation or celebration.

Can you relate? Are you one of those people that never seems to get around to doing things? Do others seem to do so much more than you do? Do they seem to be having all the fun? Achieving their goals?

That is exactly how I felt after my DVT/PE episode. Even though I knew that I had done so many amazing things and experienced so much, with what I now realised was a finite time, I started asking the following questions:

- What have I **not done** or achieved?
- How does what I have done **compare** to other people?
- Do I have **enough time** left to do everything?

Given my competitive nature, and in the absence of any other measurement mechanism, I looked for the things "everyone else" identified—the best "Top 20 *bucket list*" that I could find.

The list I picked was from a survey in 2018. Admittedly there are many such lists, but my latest online searches have confirmed that the following is still representative of common "Top 20" *bucket list* items.

1. See the Northern Lights
2. Run A Marathon
3. Take An African Safari
4. Write A Story
5. Walk The Great Wall of China
6. Learn to Play an Instrument
7. Snorkel the Barrier Reef
8. Skydive
9. Own A Dog
10. See The Pyramids of Giza
11. Learn Another Language
12. Ride a Gondola in Venice
13. Drive Across the Country
14. View Paris from the Eiffel Tower
15. Hike the Pacific Crest Trail
16. Take an Alaskan Cruise

17. See Your Favourite Band
18. Go Glamping
19. Visit Stonehenge
20. Climb Kilimanjaro (or a Big Mountain)

I soon realised that I had completed 50% of the items on the "Top 20" in their entirety, many of them more than once. Another 25% I have done in part, or something similar or with some variation. It eventually dawned on me that this information was in fact revealing an important question that I had never considered: What **have** I done and achieved?

Regardless of what I have achieved in the past, it was only as I started "measuring my life" that I began to understand how much I **had** done. It was only when I started writing this book that I truly appreciated those earlier experiences. I also came to the realisation that if I had spent all my time building a list, I would have had little time or energy left to actually do the things on the list. Planning would have taken more time than doing. Even though being the driven person that I am has sometimes led to feelings of failure and disappointment, I am so appreciative that this same drive has focused me on ***doing—not planning***.

I started asking myself other questions: ***Why*** did I do what I did? Would I do it again?

As I looked back, I identified a myriad of reasons for my choosing to do what I did and how the experiences came about. It would be exciting, it would be cool, other people want to do it so I should too. Some of the things just happened because I was at the right place at the right time, while others required preparation, determination, and discipline. Some of the experiences were relatively low risk and passive, and yet others required me to assess the risk, learn new skills, and persist with the challenge.

I began to realise that having never made a *bucket list* or consciously used the "Top 20" to drive my exploits has led to my experiences being far more expansive. Had I limited myself to a list, there are many things that I would have missed out on. Not only would I have not uncovered new things, but I would have been a great deal poorer for it. I am extremely glad I looked for new things to try and then did them.

Although I have never been driven by a list, I cannot deny that my competitive nature drove me to do things that I may not have done otherwise just because other people had done them or wanted to do so. I had to do them and aim higher.

As was the case with Carter and Edward, many of the things on the "Top 20" are related to travel and adventure. Given my enjoyment of excitement and adventure, it was not entirely unexpected that I was able to give myself credit for several items on the "Top 20." However, it generates the question: What about the people who have no desire to do those things or are unable to do so due to various constraints? Those people are no less successful than those who jump out of aeroplanes and climb mountains. For many people, not being fixated on dashing around the world, has allowed them to direct resources on what could be deemed to be less selfish endeavours.

Ultimately, I came to the realisation that how I define success is more about determining what is of value—what is most important to me and what is of value to those that I love and care about. My satisfaction hinges on finding my passion and acting on it with intention.

There can be a fine line between trying new things and trying to keep up with the Joneses; it is up to each of us to define what we value. That may vary over time and will likely be affected by those around us, particularly the ones we love. Looking back, there are several things I have done for entirely the wrong reasons, purely to prove myself in some way or because someone else was doing it. In hindsight, I could have focused my time, energy, and money on ***living my own life and on doing what I value*** versus following the dreams of others.

The DVT/PE episode opened my eyes. It did not actually make me do more; I was always someone who was motivated, driven sometimes to the point of bodily harm! What it did do was present me with the opportunity to look back and appreciate what I had experienced and achieved. It allowed me to give myself credit for having accomplished so much already. In the past, I may have considered it a self-indulgent process of chest-beating and boasting, but it turned out to be a constructive and realistic reflection. I did not do it for anyone else's benefit or to gain approval. It was an opportunity to honour myself as a person, to appreciate the gifts I had been given and to relish in what I had done with them. I am sharing it now so that others may be inspired to follow the same process—and to do so before some life-threatening event takes place.

The process also challenged me to identify where I had embarked on activities that used up valuable resources and did not contribute to what I am passionate about. I started to admit to myself that moving the goalposts and chasing meaningless goals can be demoralising. Trappist monk and scholar, Thomas Merton said, "People may spend their whole lives climbing the ladder of success only to find, once they reach the top, that the ladder is leaning against the wrong wall."

This may sound negative, as though I feel that everything I did was wrong. But it is the opposite. Everything I have done has contributed to the person that I am today. The difference is that I have more clarity about what I deem to be important and thus can be more intentional about choosing what I do. That does not mean I now have it all sorted, but I have developed a greater awareness of what I am passionate about and a commitment to make the most of every minute of my life.

Perhaps most importantly, my "life measurement process" has driven me to want to help others come to a similar realisation without having to go through a traumatic event such as my medical crisis.

There are at least two groups of people that I trust will gain from this book:

- Those of you who underestimate what you have done and keep moving the goalposts or comparing yourself to others. Whilst it is good to keep dreaming and growing, it is equally as important to count your blessings, take stock of what you have done, and use that to propel you into the future.
- Those of you who think you can do things later when you have the time or money to do so. When you are fitter. When you have a partner. When your children have left home. When you have fewer work commitments. When you have retired. One never knows what could happen. In my case it was DVT/PE, for others, it was Covid. Do not assume there will be time. To use a cliché—Carpe Diem, seize the day. Do not put off things you really want to do as you may run out of time to do them.

In both instances, I encourage and challenge you to figure out how to make the most of every second of your earthly life. To celebrate your successes, to take action instead of planning to do so, to focus on what is of value to you and those you love, and to do it.

You may notice a predisposition towards adventures and travel in this book. In the first instance, this was because I started my life measurement process using the "Top 20" list as a basis; as in the movie, this inventory is biased towards globetrotting exploits. In addition, the selection of stories has been driven by the interest that I have received from others who have been inspired by my experiences.

Just as my stories have inspired people to try new things, some of the stories in this book may do just that for you. You may well be tempted by the specific experiences described and wish to do them. Perhaps reading my stories will be sufficient to satisfy your curiosity about the experience. Some things are worth enjoying vicariously through someone else. Much as we may like to, we cannot do everything. Instead, we can choose to share our passions and stories, living through the experiences of others and letting them do the same through us.

When you read the stories of my adventures, I encourage you not to think of them as a finite list of things you should do. Not everyone values the same adventurous endeavours that I have focused on. Your idea of being adventurous may be learning to swim in the sea or to drive a car. What you value most could be paying off your mortgage.

If you gain nothing else from this book, I hope you are encouraged to live your own life and live it to the fullest—whatever that means to you.

I was tempted to give you a list of actions and processes to help you identify and follow your passions, but that approach seems to go against the idea of **kicking out** the *bucket list*. It would revert, at least in part, to applying a formula or using someone else's approach to living your life. Instead, I am going to let my stories excite, inspire, or bore you and leave you to decide what impact you would like them to have. Although there are a few things for you to ponder at the end of each chapter, it is up to you how you use these ideas. They are there to prompt you to trigger your own memories or to make you dream about the possibilities. They are designed to help you envision what could be and take action to make it so. The opportunities are infinite. The only thing that limits you is your own imagination. As I take you through the steps in my life measurement process, I encourage you to reflect on your own life.

THE FINITE LIST
THE "TOP 20"

The first step in my life measurement process focused on the "Top 20," those endeavours that could be deemed big-ticket items, those popular things that would frequently make their way to the proverbial *bucket list*. The "Top 20" list seemed a convenient way to measure my life. It is finite, so it is easy to determine what is in and what is out. It is a list of the experiences and achievements that many would use to measure themselves, to determine the value or success of their own lives. The incompletion of the "Top 20" would indicate that they failed in some way.

Hence, evaluating my success with the "Top 20" seemed a logical starting point in my quest for seeing how I stacked up against other people and what the rest of the population deemed to be noteworthy pursuits.

By reflecting upon my adventures and experiences in this way, I am not promoting the "Top 20" or any other *bucket list*; I am merely using this list as a starting point to consider the things I have experienced in my life and to prompt you to embark on a similar process of reflection.

4

Done and Dusted

The first step in my life measurement process was to identify those things on the "Top 20" list that I had completed. As I ticked off items on the "Top 20," I was able to appreciate my experiences and celebrate my successes. I was able to relish in the thought that I had done a large number of those things that many others on our planet have done or would like to do. I was able to celebrate those that I had accomplished rather than focus on the things that I had not done.

Run A Marathon

Many people are under the impression that any run is a marathon. By definition, a marathon is 42.195 km (approximately 26 miles). The idea for the modern marathon was inspired by the legend of the ancient Greek messenger Pheidippides who, in 490 B.C., raced from the site of Marathon to Athens (a distance of about 40 kilometres) with the news of a significant Greek victory over an invading army of Persians. After making his announcement, the exhausted messenger collapsed and died. To commemorate his dramatic run, the distance of the marathon at the inaugural Modern Olympic Games in Athens in 1896 was set at 40 km.

At the 1908 Olympic Games in London, the course was extended, allegedly to accommodate the British royal family. As the story goes, Queen Alexandra requested that the race start on the lawn of Windsor Castle (so the littlest royals could watch from the window of their nursery) and finish in front of the royal box at the Olympic stadium—a distance of 26.2 miles (26 miles and 385 yards). The random boost in mileage ended up sticking and, in 1921, the length for a marathon was formally standardised at 42.195 km (26.2 miles). The Olympic Marathon and any marathon events throughout the world are strictly measured at this distance.

Although running a marathon is no average feat, there exists a misconception that running one is no longer that impressive; that somehow making it through 42.195 km on foot in a morning has become easier than it used to be. Maybe that is because I hear so many people having completed a 5 km *run* saying they have run a *marathon*. (You may be hearing my sigh.) A 5 km run is precisely that, a 5 km run. The same with a 10 km run. Even a half marathon is exactly that—half of a marathon, at 21.0975 km. The only run that can be called a marathon is one with a distance of 42.195 km.

In an article published in November 2022 by the Marathon Handbook—an organisation founded with the express purpose of helping people run far—it was concluded that only 0.17% of the world's population has run a marathon. The research was based on a comprehensive mapping of global running participation carried out by RunRepeat, a renowned group of running fanatics, in 2019. The analysis covered 107.9 million race results from more than 70,000 running events over the course of 22 years (1986 to 2018).

As already mentioned, I grew up competing with two much older brothers, so I had to climb higher, play harder, and go faster than a boy—and an older boy at that—to simply keep up. I was a fit competitor who excelled in multiple sports. But I could not run. Or so I thought.

As a child, if I tried to go for a run, I would be out of breath before the corner. "I can't run" became a mantra. My husband is the natural runner in the family. Before and soon after we were married, I would kiss him goodbye as he left for his morning run. At events, I would sit at the finish line, waiting for him to come in. Until one day, I looked at the profile of those coming across the line—young, old, thin, fat— and figured I could do it too.

I started out small. I puffed my way through 1 km at a time, slowly increasing to my first 5 km race! I made it up to 10 km and felt very proud of myself. "No, I'll never do a marathon," I told myself. "I'm not interested in that."

One day, in the lead-up to the 2001 marathon in Canberra, Australia, I made what would turn out to be a life-changing decision. Four days before the event, I decided to do the full marathon. (I need to clarify that whilst the decision to run the event was last minute, I had done the necessary training. As a member of the Sydney Striders Running Club, I had struggled through months of long runs with support by my side in the form of other very experienced marathoners.) My husband had already registered for the race and was encouraging me to give it a go. My resolve to keep up with others was likely the final factor that drove me to enter. At the registration desk, surrounded by other competitors, my determination not to be left out gave me the final incentive I needed to complete my registration.

On marathon day, I had the time of my life. Other club members encouraged me along the route. I had no expectations of myself so was happy to take it easy and enjoy the journey. As my race entry was a last-minute decision, very few people knew I was doing it, and I did not feel the pressure I would have felt to perform had all my family and friends been checking my progress. (At that point in time, the activity tracking software Strava did not exist and there was no online live tracking of the event, so no one would have been able to follow my run or see how well I had performed unless I chose to let them know.) Apart from a blister on my baby toe, I had a fabulous day out, finishing in a reasonable, albeit not spectacular, time of 4 hours and 6 minutes.

Only after completing my first marathon, did I realise that I enjoyed the companionship of training with my husband and the thrill of completing something that I found tough. Since then, running has been addictive and anyone meeting me today would not believe that at one time I did not run ... that I thought I could not run. Since that first marathon in Canberra, I have completed numerous marathons across Australia, joined 44,000 people from around the world on the Champs Elysée to complete the Paris Marathon, and navigated the cobblestones to complete the Florence Marathon. Regular running has also made me fit enough to be able to do things when the opportunity presented itself, including taking part in the Vancouver Half Marathon and the Banff Half Marathon during an extended trip to Canada.

Have you completed a marathon? If so, kudos to you! If not, is it something you aspire to do? If not, drop it, let go, do not stick it on some list of items that you may never do. But if it is something you would like to do ... take action towards that goal. Perhaps join a running group for support. It will take time and effort, but as I found out, it may not be impossible even if you once thought it to be so.

Take an African Safari

Growing up in South Africa in a family that was animal and bird-mad, meant that a trip to the Kruger National Park was an annual occurrence. The park is one of Africa's largest game reserves (19,485 square kilometres). Its high density of wild animals includes the Big Five: lions, leopards, rhinos, elephants, and buffalos. Hundreds of other mammals make their home here, as do diverse bird species such as vultures, eagles, and storks. Mountains, bush plains, and tropical forests are all part of the landscape.

I feel that I need to explain what an African Safari means to a family of avid photographers and future game rangers. Five members of our family piled into the family sedan, with me as the youngest being sandwiched in the middle of the back seat between my older brothers. There was no paid expert guide to seek out the animals for us, no luxury lodges—just clouds of dust and hours of looking for wild animals. Not a zoo, but an experience of looking for the animals in their territory and only seeing them when they chose to be seen. Stopping to look through binoculars at an anthill that someone was convinced had moved or a rock that most certainly could have been an elephant. My brothers would tell me to go to sleep in the back of the car making a promise that doing so would enable us to see a lion. I have since realised that this was a way of trying to keep me quiet rather than a belief that I could bring on the good luck of seeing the most elusive animals.

For some reason, the impala—a medium-sized antelope—became known as *Glenda's buck*. *Buck* is the zoological term for several animals, including deer, hares, and goats—but in South Africa, it tends to be used to describe what would commonly be known in other parts of the world as antelope. I can only assume that an impala was the first animal I ever saw in the wild due to their prevalence. In spite of the fact that they are rampant, I remain fond of the pretty, reddish creatures.

Many an early morning was spent leaving the rondavel (a traditional circular African dwelling with a conical thatched roof) at the camp to venture out on a game drive with my dad at the wheel. Once the sun rises high in the sky, the animals become difficult to see amongst the shade of the trees. Early in the morning, they are much more likely to wander alongside the road or visit a watering hole for a drink or a bath. After a few hours of game viewing, we would return to camp where my mother would have prepared a breakfast of fried eggs and bully beef (a variety of meat made from finely minced corned beef in a small amount of gelatin). For some reason, bully beef was something to be eaten at the game reserve and was never consumed at any other time.

As a child, being part of a family that was besotted over African wildlife, I had often heard of the Serengeti. A 30,000 square km expanse in Tanzania, the Serengeti hosts the second largest terrestrial mammal migration in the world, which helps secure it as one of the Seven Natural Wonders of Africa and as one of the ten natural travel wonders of the world. The Serengeti is also renowned for its large lion population and is one of the best places to observe a pride of lions in their natural environment.

Travel from South Africa to Tanzania was limited, expensive, and not always safe, so it was never on the cards. In 2014, after having been in flat Australia for almost 20 years and missing Africa and the mountains, Walter and I decided to make a trip to climb Mount Kilimanjaro in Tanzania. Given the proximity to the Serengeti, we decided to add that to the trip. I thought I was dreaming. I truly could not believe that I was in this place that I had heard so much about as a child.

Our guide was continually shocked at the fact that he was not required to spend his time seeking out the Big Five. The term "Big Five" originally referred to the difficulty in hunting the animals, not their size or level of importance. But for some reason, most tourists think that the lion, leopard, rhino, elephant, and African buffalo are the only animals that must be seen on safari. That if they are not found, the safari has been a waste, and the guide has failed them. Sadly, this at times means that a game-viewing experience in the wild turns into an outing that one may expect at the local city zoo. I am someone with the attention span of a fish, I cannot sit through an entire movie, but when it comes to wildlife, I can spend hours identifying the pretty lilac-breasted rollers (birds) or sitting at waterholes listening to the noise of the bush and waiting for wildlife to make an appearance as they make their way for a drink.

We had not timed our visit to the Serengeti to take advantage of the annual animal migration from the neighbouring Masai Mara—Kenya's National Reserve equivalent to the Serengeti. With early rains that year, we were fortunate to catch the early days of seeing the plains fill with zebra and blue wildebeest as they arrived in search of food and water. Each day there were more and more lines of these animals making their way across the savanna, to the pleasure of the hungry-looking lions that had been short of food since the previous season.

On the way to the Serengeti, we visited the Ngorongoro Crater, the world's largest inactive, intact and unfilled volcanic caldera. The crater, which formed when a large volcano exploded and collapsed on itself two to three million years ago, is 610 metres (2,000 feet) deep and its floor covers 260 square km (100 square miles). Now, the crater is teaming with wildlife, so much so that it feels a little like a gigantic zoo. In 2013 the crater was voted one of the Seven Natural Wonders of Africa, adding to the list of remarkable natural wonders that the organisation, Seven Natural Wonders, aims to protect.

As the saying goes, you can take someone out of the bush but you cannot take the bush out of someone. Seeking out animals in their own habitat played a significant part in my early life.

Have you been on an African Safari? Or a similar adventure where animals were the focus? If so, what was the highlight? Does the idea of searching out wildlife interest you, either on a small or large safari? If you would like to maximise the number of animals you see, you may wish to sign up with a guide rather than rely on your own game-spotting skills.

Learn to Play an Instrument

Some people may say that the recorder is not really an instrument. It is something given to children to blow and make a noise. So, my experience of learning to play the plastic version of this little instrument when I was six years old may not even count as learning an instrument to some people—let alone a big-ticket achievement. (I am unsure if I should admit it, but I did play it my whole school career, and was even the leader of the recorder band during my final year.) The biggest benefit of playing the recorder was that it was instrumental (pun intended) in teaching me to read music, which was not only useful when I sang, but it led to my learning to play the piano.

I am not sure what my initial motivations were to play the piano. Maybe it was something that I was yet to master, or maybe it was to keep up with someone else. Regardless of the motivation, my parents graciously purchased a second-hand upright and paid a considerable amount of money for lessons.

Unfortunately, my piano-playing ambitions were relatively short-lived, with many factors working against my initial ambitions. The practice pianos at school were in a dark, damp, cold building at the bottom of the boarding school gardens, so I was not particularly enthusiastic about spending time there. A contributing factor may also have been that I was distracted by the debating society, jazz and tap dancing, tennis, swimming, and art classes. However, despite the distractions and my lack of motivation, I did become fairly proficient at playing Beethoven's *Für Elise*.

Whilst my piano followed me from home to home in South Africa and to Sydney, Australia, it met its demise when it could no longer be tuned. Pianos consist of an intricate set of moving parts and regular moves or incorrect moving techniques can dislodge some or all of the components. If a piano is old or neglected, it might be unable to be tuned. After spending copious amounts of money transporting this beautiful wooden piece of furniture across the globe, I accepted that my well-travelled instrument was no longer able to be tuned.

In hindsight, I should have left the piano in South Africa instead of ruining it by transporting it across the sea. If I am truly honest with myself, maybe I should have resigned myself to enjoying the music of others and not felt the desire to do what others were doing. Perhaps my time would have been better spent focusing more attention on one or more of my other pursuits. It certainly would have saved copious amounts of money - that of my parents buying the piano, tuition fees, and hiring removalists that could tackle the large instrument and transport it to its many homes, and eventually to its demise.

So, one may say I ticked off this item. I found that learning the recorder led to learning another instrument and gave me a deep appreciation of different types of music. But I would certainly not call myself a musician. I did not do it justice. What was missing? Passion? Practice?

If you have learned an instrument, what made you give the pursuit the attention it deserved? Many people learn to play an instrument because their parents wish them to. Was there pressure for you to learn? If so, did this impact your level of commitment?

Snorkel the Barrier Reef

When I was in my fourth year of primary school, friends of my parents gave me a gift of a wooden ruler. In fact, I still have said measuring device. What was particularly significant about this object was that they brought it back from a trip to Australia. For a young child living in South Africa, Australia was another world. We had little or no TV to expose us to overseas news or documentaries. The South African government chose not to provide black-and-white viewing to the population, so television was only introduced in 1976 when colour television was becoming dominant. The country was also under global sanctions because of the laws of apartheid, which further limited information. Our worldview was largely restricted to what we learned in the classroom. A ruler with photos of Hayman Island, one of the Whitsunday Islands bordering Australia's Great Barrier Reef, was certainly not something any of my friends owned.

Little did I know at that point that not only would I get to snorkel on the Barrier Reef and spend weeks sailing around the Whitsunday Islands, but I would also get to stay on Hayman Island and swim in its famous pool depicted on my ruler.

Prior to immigrating to Australia, on a holiday to visit my brother in Sydney, Walter and I booked a short side excursion to Mackay, one of the gateways to the Barrier Reef. We took a bumpy boat ride out to the reef to try our hand at snorkelling; despite most of the passengers around us being seasick, we managed to keep our nausea at bay. The time spent jumping off the man-made platform in the middle of the sea over the reef was worth the travel discomfort. Being amongst the fish in their territory was serene and a wonderful reminder of the wonder of God's creation. (It was the amazing experience of swimming amongst the brightly coloured coral fish and turquoise parrot fish in the clear azure water that eventually enabled me to convince my water-averse husband to try scuba diving.)

Not only did I inadvertently tick off the seemingly much-aspired item of snorkelling the Barrier Reef, but the adventure led to hours spent underwater amongst the coral, fish, turtles and sharks, not only in Australia, but in other areas of the world as well. Drift diving off a boat at Aliwal Shoal off the east coast of South Africa was an easy way to enjoy being under the water and at the same time expend very little effort. The boat would drop us off and then pick us up at the position to which we had drifted.

Completing my advanced diver certificate at Sodwana Bay (near the Mozambique border with South Africa) taught me how to share air underwater. This was important as I seemed to run out of air underwater much sooner than everyone else. I was told that the more experienced I became and the more I relaxed, the less air I would use up. In all my years of diving, this has never been the case. My competitive nature made this fact difficult to accept at times as I thought I should improve and use less air like other experienced divers. Fortunately, it did not stop me from diving and it was only years later after undergoing tests for breathing issues, that I discovered that I have a low lung capacity. The cause has not been identified, but at least now I have an explanation for the mystery.

A week at a dive resort in Fiji was the pinnacle of my diving experience. It is the only time in my life that I have spent a full week surrounded by other divers and dedicated to enjoying the sport without any pressure of passing tests. The diving was easy as we would hop on a dive boat set up for the express purpose of conveying people to various dive sites. As most of the diving was done at less than 12 metres below sea level, the light from the sun reflected on the fish and corals, revealing vibrant shades of yellow, blue and pink.

My most memorable dive was the day Walter and I *almost* entered New Zealand waters … by mistake. We were planning a dive off a yacht moored in the beautiful Butterfly Bay on the top of Hook Island in the Whitsunday Islands (and incidentally just near Hayman Island). After putting on all our diving gear, we hopped into the water. Before we had even thought of going down, we looked across and realised how far we had already been washed away from our boat.

As we were alone on the yacht, we were very fortunate that the old Ragamuffin, a retired 70-foot, single-hulled racing yacht designed for the Admiral's Cup (an international yachting regatta) was out on a sightseeing cruise. They threw out a rope that we could grab hold of. As we were dragged behind, their engine labouring against the extremely strong current, it felt like hours before we were eventually safely on board our own vessel.

I still enjoy snorkelling when given the opportunity. As for diving – I admit to feeling some envy when I hear others have been spending time under the water. However, my passion has waned, the value-for-effort ratio has decreased and so I need to acknowledge that diving is no longer a priority for me and be satisfied with other people's stories or my own snorkelling experiences. Each dive takes considerable time to set up and test equipment, to access the dive site, and to clean the gear afterwards.

Also, if you have flown from somewhere for the dive, there may be a limitation on how soon afterwards you can leave. Diving increases nitrogen levels in your blood and these levels need to be brought down before flying otherwise it can lead to what is commonly called "The Bends" (*decompression sickness*)—which can be fatal.

Do you snorkel or dive? Have you experienced the wonder of gliding amongst the big and small creatures of the sea? If not, and you have always wanted to, perhaps it is time to do so. If you are lukewarm, try snorkelling if given the opportunity. Snorkelling requires very little equipment or time to master whereas diving demands a significant financial investment in equipment and training to acquire the required qualifications.

Own a Dog

This is one of those items that in itself does not seem like it should be a big item on a *bucket list* as the initial purchase or adoption of a dog might not require much effort. However, many people do not fully appreciate that owning a dog is a long-term commitment or they underestimate the amount of work needed to look after a dog.

I checked off this item without even thinking about it. As you may have already picked up, my family is animal mad. Not only wildlife, but anything with four legs, or with wings, or that slithers. So, growing up with a dog in the family was a done deal. Sally, a wheaten Labrador, was with me most of my young life and we enjoyed many a happy hour playing in the garden and even swimming in the sea. It was hard to watch her suffer from hip dysplasia—a common ailment of Labradors—and eventually, we had to bid her farewell.

Not only was I blessed with owning a dog, but over the years, my childhood house was also home to rabbits, rosy-faced lovebirds, a cockatiel named Tinkles, barn owls, fish, hamsters, snakes—and mice to feed the snakes. On one occasion, my brother arrived home from his vacation job at the local vet on a horse, but sadly my parents made him take it back. (A half-acre property was probably not sufficient space for a paddock.)

Having lived in apartments during my early years in Australia and now being a travelling nomad, the only animals I have kept of late were fish. A lifestyle choice!

If you have looked after a pet, what did you find rewarding or challenging about doing so? If you have not done so, is now the time for you to take on the commitment of a dog or some other creature?

Learn Another Language

I grew up in a country with multiple languages. In South Africa, at least thirty-five indigenous languages are spoken, ten of which are now official languages: Ndebele, Pedi, Sotho, Swati, Tsonga, Tswana,

Venda, Xhosa, Zulu, and Afrikaans. The eleventh official language is English, which is the primary language used in parliamentary and state discourse, though all official languages are equal in legal status, and unofficial languages are protected under the Constitution of South Africa.

When I was growing up, South Africa was a bilingual country. Although the indigenous languages were spoken, English and Afrikaans were the official languages. Television programs spanned the two languages, all products were labelled in two languages, notices and signboards were printed in both, and we had to learn both at school.

So, learning two languages was natural and I was able to accomplish this with very little effort on my part. I studied French as part of my final high school certificate. Learning to speak, read, and write French has held me in good stead for all the travelling I have done in South America and Europe in later years. Not only was my language skill in French useful when I visited France, but the language is also similar enough to Italian and Spanish to assist me in understanding the conversation. I have even been able to draw on my years of Afrikaans study; with its origins in Dutch, I can communicate with those from The Netherlands fairly well. It has some similarities to German which means that if someone speaks very slowly and simply, I can usually follow the gist of the conversation.

If you originate from Europe, you probably already understand and even speak multiple languages. For the rest of us, learning to speak another language is a big accomplishment. As with most things, it becomes more difficult to learn a language as one gets older so I am grateful for the opportunity to learn multiple languages before I became an adult. I am currently motivated to speak Italian as I am living in Italy and need to understand it to be able to conduct the typical day-to-day transactions of ordering coffee and buying bread.

My passion has increased now that I am surrounded by the language I wish to master.

Are you proficient in multiple languages? If so, congratulations. If not, do you have a desire to learn a new language? Are you up for the challenge and effort to do so? If so, good luck, bonne chance (French), sterkte (Afrikaans), buona fortuna (Italian), buene suerte (Spanish), or ngikufisela inhlanhla (Zulu).

View Paris from the Eiffel Tower

Little did I know that my decision to choose French instead of Geography for my school certificate would have me accomplishing something that so many people dream of. A visit to Paris! Four days in the *City of Love*. Do not get me wrong, I enjoyed learning the language and was fortunately pretty good at it. But being immersed in a language and surrounded by its ambient culture is certainly the best way to learn, so when I was offered a place on a school trip, it was the opportunity of a lifetime. Looking back, I am so grateful to my parents for providing the funds for me to go. My dad was retired and they were already stretched by my private school fees. I often wonder whether this trip, my first outside of Southern Africa, was instrumental in the development of my desire to explore the world.

I did not get to the very top of the Eiffel Tower as the final section was closed due to maintenance. I did, however, manage to ascend in the lift to the first level from where I could see the breathtaking views across the *arrondissements* (districts) of Paris.

The funny thing is that the adventure nearly did not take place. First, our French teacher and planned chaperone discovered she was pregnant and was forced to pull out. Finding a replacement teacher from a nearby school did not prove too difficult, given the lady in question was an avid traveller and a self-confessed Francophile.

Problem solved! Then, the day before we were meant to depart, all our passports were lost! Somehow, they had disappeared in transit from the French consulate to our travel agent after being stamped with the required visas. You may not realise what this meant! In Australia, we have managed to get a passport in a couple of hours, but in South Africa, a couple of months is more likely—and that is if you are extremely lucky. So, it was an amazing feat for someone to pull a rabbit out of the hat, get us replacement passports and new visas and have us on the plane only a few days after we were due to leave. Imagine, I could have missed out on that view!

I have been blessed to visit Paris a couple of times since, enjoying the twinkling of the Eiffel Tower at night and standing underneath the mammoth steel structure. I even have photos of me running past during the Paris Marathon. Strangely, I have never been up the famous tower again, choosing instead to ascend the lesser-known Montparnasse Tower, which affords views just as splendid with fewer people and at a much lower cost.

I think there would be few people who would say Paris is not on their list of places to visit. If you have not been there, maybe the question is, where does it sit on your list? Are you going to make it happen in the next year? Five years? If you do go, what would you like to do there? Would you prioritise the view from the Eiffel Tower?

Go Glamping

It seems that everyone has a very different view of what glamping is. Some people think that going to the caravan park by the beach, armed with a camping stove, portable toilet and fridge could be deemed as glamping. Others expect glamping to be a hotel room in canvas, complete with a flushing toilet, four-poster bed, and room service. Either way, it does appear to be a fad that many people are wanting to do and a niche that numerous businesses are taking advantage of.

Let me explain my opinion on the matter. I am a person of extremes. If I am going camping, it is mud huts, waterfalls for showering, and long drop toilets dug in the ground. Otherwise, it is five stars all the way! So, if I am going glamping, I expect something like I experienced on my visit to the Serengeti. We were provided hot water for the shower; staff would bring it across in a large container and fill the shower receptacle. The tent also contained a flushing toilet, a huge dressing room, two bedrooms, and a living area. The butler would arrive outside the canvas flap each morning with tea in silver service. He would also collect us in the evening for gin and tonic around the campfire. (We soon realised the reason for the nightly escort when one evening he shone his torchlight into the eyes of a large buffalo two metres from our tent!)

By my definition, our accommodation in the Amazon Rainforest in Peru was borderline glamping, but it was extremely unique. The comfortable queen size beds covered in crisp white linen did have nets to protect us from the mosquitoes, however with no canvas, wood, bricks or reeds to separate us from the outdoors, I was grateful that we avoided having any unwelcome visitors in our rooms—such as spiders and snakes. Particularly as our single kerosene lamp would not have provided us with sufficient light to see the creatures as we strolled to the ensuite.

Although not always glamping, seeking out unique accommodation has become one of my fetishes. Over the years, I have stayed in caves, fountains and palazzos in Italy, a dome house, a gypsy caravan, and a treehouse in Australia. I have slept in converted churches and even a renovated stable. Sleeping in open swags under the stars in the Australian outback was memorable, but certainly not glamping. Swags are compact sleeping spaces and beds designed to provide some protection from the elements when camping. The open swags meant that we were able to stare at the stars without the limits of a tent roof.

What is your definition of glamping? What interesting accommodation have you stayed in? Or do you just prefer good old hotel/motel rooms?

Climb Kilimanjaro

The camping experience when climbing Kilimanjaro probably cannot be described as glamping, even though we had an entourage of thirteen people to support just two of us—one of those thirteen people was allocated the job of setting up the toilet tent containing a plastic bucket. The food was remarkable. Our cook, Barrack (given it was during the time of President Obama, we nicknamed him Mr President) even managed to put together a delicious crispy pizza at 4000 metres above sea level. He carried dozens of eggs on his back every day as he navigated the steep paths up the mountain.

One of the seven highest peaks in the world at an altitude of 5,892 metres, Kilimanjaro is the highest mountain that can be hiked— rather than requiring mountaineering skills and equipment such as ropes, harnesses and crampons. There are five different paths available and the length of the itinerary varies.

Fitness levels are important to be able to cover the distance as it is all uphill. However, the main consideration in determining the length of the climb and which path to take was which combination was the best option to avoid altitude sickness. Altitude sickness is caused by ascending too rapidly, which does not allow the body enough time to adjust to reduced oxygen and changes in air pressure. Symptoms include headache, vomiting, insomnia, and reduced performance and coordination.

There have been many studies and theories on the risk factors for altitude sickness but there is no conclusive evidence on who is likely to suffer more. Fitness does not seem to be a factor. Former tennis star Martina Navratilova was hospitalised after her attempt to climb Kilimanjaro was cut short when she experienced high-altitude pulmonary edema (HAPE), a potentially fatal form of altitude sickness. HAPE is a dangerous build-up of fluid in the lungs. The treatment for HAPE is immediate descent.

Walter and I were both born and grew up in Johannesburg, South Africa at a relatively high altitude of 1,753 metres and this factor may have been in our favour. We have also hiked to a height of above 4,000 metres in the Andes and been to Everest Base Camp at an altitude of 5,364 metres without succumbing to the illness, so we were fairly confident. That said, we chose to play it safe with a slightly longer itinerary, determining that it was unlikely that we would return to Kilimanjaro if we failed at this attempt.

In addition to meeting the primary objective of acclimatising to the altitude changes, this choice did mean that we had plenty of time each day to relax at our camp after only needing a few hours to walk from the previous night's resting place. It also amused our guide as he was convinced that we could have done it in at least two days less. He was happy—as the slower journey made his job significantly easier.

Following four days of climbing, I woke up at midnight with the rain falling gently on our tent. This was our morning to summit the mountain! After dressing with three layers on the bottom and five on top, we went to the meal tent for a very early "breakfast"—more like a midnight snack. The full moon and dusting of snow greeting us when we exited the canvas door were breathtaking.

We trudged up the steep switchbacks in the dark, blissfully unaware of the steep drop-off next to the path. The water in our hydration bladders had frozen, despite the special insulation sleeve we had used to cover them. Fortunately, our guide was carrying a large thermos of hot chocolate which gave us both energy and liquid during our short stop under an overhang on the way up.

Mount Kilimanjaro is a dormant volcano in Tanzania. It has three volcanic cones: Kibo, Mawenzi, and Shira. It is the highest mountain in Africa and the highest single free-standing mountain in the world: 5,895 metres above sea level and about 4,900 metres above its plateau base. To reach the actual summit of Kilimanjaro, Uhuru Peak (5,895 meters/19,341 feet), we went via Gilman's Point and then on to Stella Point at an altitude of 5,756 meters. Stella Point is situated at the edge of the crater rim. It was good to have some checkpoints along the way to give us a sense of achievement and time for a breather.

The final climb up the ridge to the summit was slow and cold. Our guide had timed it perfectly, and just as we reached the peak, we could see the sun rising out of the mist in the valley and over the surrounding glaciers. Thankfully, the altitude had not affected us in the way that it does so many people, so we could have stayed on the summit for a while. But despite all the layers of clothing—and additional down mittens, buffs and beanies—we could not bear the icy cold wind. Soon we were sliding down the scree slopes to the bottom.

We were given a choice between sliding more or less straight down or trudging back and forth along the switchbacks. The switchbacks were great on the way up as it allowed time for acclimatisation. A vertical ascent is taxing on the lungs and legs. However, switchbacks do make the walk further. Besides taking so much longer to walk, why would anyone want to miss the fun of screeching down the scree slopes? Using our hiking poles like ski poles, we wove our way through the accumulation of loose stones and rocky debris lying on the slope. The risks of falling were fairly high and coming down on the sharp stones would have been painful. My boots were full of stones and dust by the time I reached the bottom. But the exhilaration of the journey and the reward of getting down so quickly far outweighed the risk. The congratulatory welcome we received from our team when we arrived at camp for breakfast was the icing on the cake. They were relieved and excited that we had made it to the summit and back to a safe altitude.

Having reached the summit of the highest free-standing mountain in the world I am happy to admit that I am not going to pursue anything higher. I do not have the desire nor need to risk further life and limb (and copious amounts of money) to take on the summit of Mount Everest, which would be the next challenge.

Are you fit and able to persist through adversity? Have you experienced what it feels like to be at high altitudes? These are considerations when choosing a trip to Kili. Do you want to experience the elation and satisfaction of making it to the top and seeing the reddening glaciers as the sun rises over them?

Summary

We run the risk of thinking only about those items we have not done and not revelling in those that we have. I may have started measuring my life when something out of my control happened to me, but it was only as I prepared to write this book, that I realised that I had inadvertently ticked off more than half of the things that so many people seem to want to do (using the "Top 20" list as a yardstick). I realised that in some instances I may have enjoyed the kudos others had given me at the time, but that the benefits of this acclaim were typically short-lived. This process of revisiting my adventures provided me with an opportunity to appreciate what I had done, not only for the glory—but for my own satisfaction. The process prompted me to consider those things that were similar in nature to the "Top 20" even if they were not quite the "real deal."

POINTS FOR REFLECTION

Look back at the list of the Top 20 in Chapter 3 and identify if there are any items that you could say you have completed. Celebrate them!

Which gave you the most satisfaction? Why?

5

Not Quite the Real Deal

I have experienced a number of things that I believe could be considered comparable to the "Top 20." Frequently, these experiences have satisfied my curiosity, and in some instances, I would rate the experience better than had I done it in its purest form. They were less touristy, a better bang for the buck, or just much more fun. I was happy to include them in my celebration of things I have done even if they could only be measured as "Almost Done."

Write a Story

I find it interesting that writing a story is on the "Top 20"—that it is such a highly desirable endeavour by a large number of people. One could debate what one means by a "story." I guess many of us have written essays during our educational years, so a large number of people can tick this one off in its simplest form. However, I am not convinced that is what is meant by the aspiration to write a story.

As I travelled extensively and collected photo after photo, friends and family asked about my trips and I started wondering how to share. What was the best way to allow people to read as much or as little as they wanted? (After all, who wants to go through the family slide show?) That is how the idea of a travel blog was born. These days, many of us write articles and blogs to be posted online, so maybe that ticks the box.

That said, for me, I really want it to be a novel, something with the longevity of one of Agatha Christie's mysteries. For this reason, even though I have written this book of stories, I have included this as an almost done rather than something that I have completed.

Having the intention is great, doing it is not always easy. Theodore Roosevelt once said that "nothing worth having comes easy." The harder it is the more we tend to value it. It is about overcoming adversity. Challenging fear.

For me, fear of heights, speed, or doing something adventurous does not trigger fear. As I am fit, most things requiring physical capability do not either. The most terrifying thing for me is a fear of failure! I tend to withdraw from things that require a response or approval from others. I am unaware of a similar feeling as a child—maybe because I was always at the top—but over the years I developed a fear of failure. Particularly where success is dependent on other people, on their opinions. If I do not do it, they will not see me fail.

Writing this book has been one of my biggest personal challenges. It was something I considered for years, encouraged by colleagues, friends and family to do it. Even as I completed the final chapter, I still worried—what if no one likes it, what if it is not published … what if …? But I look back on the process and realise that irrespective of what happens next, I have been successful. I have thoroughly enjoyed the process of looking back on my life and relishing the blessings that

I have received. I have refused to overanalyse everything, but rather I took one step at a time. To not worry about what may happen, to not try and control everything—but to just do it. In much the same way as I have always embarked on activities and adventures.

Who would have thought – I was prepared to risk life and limb to climb mountains and jump off cliffs but was terrified of writing this book. I needed to challenge my thinking, risk failure, and trust my gut. For a period, I stopped writing. I wondered why I was doing it. I watched the success of others and thought that I just could not do it.

It took an attitude change for me to implement some of the things I have told others over the years. I needed the prodding, support and coaching of others to help me through the process.

I believe that this experience has not only allowed me to overcome some of my fears, but I honestly believe I will be a much better coach. Although in the past I have been able to inspire and motivate people, I know that the extra empathy I have developed through fighting my own demons will stand me in good stead to be even more helpful. Coming alongside others, encouraging and at the same time sharing my own struggles, will open a new door for me and enable me to help so many more people in an even greater way.

It may not be a novel, but I am more than satisfied having taken this step. Perhaps my definition of writing a story has changed and soon I may consider moving it to the "done" pile.

Should I be looking for your novel to hit the shelves anytime soon? There are plenty of book coaches, author forums, and other support systems in place to help you. I encourage you to make use of them.

Ride a Gondola in Venice

I would be lying if I said that I had not watched those good looking, buff Italian men in their striped shirts using their oars to propel and guide their well-known, flat-bottomed boats through the canals of Venice, wishing for a trip on said vessel, my husband nestled beside me in the sumptuous satin cushions. There is something romantic about the idea, especially if one adds to the dream a sunset serenade.

The adverts say "enjoy an authentically Venetian experience" or "float along the serene canals of Venice." I am not entirely sure what makes an authentic experience, but I have it on fairly good authority that the locals do not pay the required tourist prices for this experience. And where the allure of serenity may have been true in years gone by, it is by no means the case now. The last time I was in Venice, the waterways were jam-packed with boats—so full that the boats could barely move. The romantic serenity was drowned out by gondoliers shouting and the smacking sound of crafts knocking against each other.

There is a way to have a short thrill and live like a local for just a single coin. The so-called gondola ferry—in Italian, the gondola *traghetto*—is a quick way to cross the Grand Canal in Venice when there are no nearby bridges. As you may know, there are only four bridges along the Grand Canal and several points where there is no way to cross. You are forced to walk all the way around to reach the other side. If it is high season with big crowds, good luck fighting through the masses! That is where the gondola *traghetto* comes in.

I am not in any way playing down the real gondola ride experience. The classic gondola ride is made with an embellished gondola and has a totally different atmosphere than the gondola ferry. It is also more relaxing as you do not have to remain standing as you do on the *traghetto*. One day, I may take the opportunity to do it in style in the more lavish vessel. For now, I am content to settle for having had a ball on this crossing gondola ride.

Would you consider taking a special trip to Venice to go on a gondola? If you go to Venice, is it a high priority for you to go on one? Or has your interest in the traghetto been piqued and you may consider that instead?

Take an Alaskan Cruise

Given this experience makes it to the "Top 20" list, it must be something that a large percentage of the population aspires to doing. I cannot say that one of my lifetime dreams was to take an Alaskan cruise. Not that I disliked the idea of travelling through some of the world's most remote, untamed wilderness with up-close viewings of wildlife such as brown bears and whale sightings. It was just that I had not given it much thought. By the same token, I was fascinated by those giant black and white sea creatures known as Orcas.

Although not able to make any claim on completing this "Top 20" item, I have had two journeys on the water that I feel are comparable to an Alaskan Cruise and could be deemed equally significant.

The first of these is a ferry crossing travelling north through the Inside Passage from Vancouver Island, Canada on the way to Alaska.

Sailing the Inside Passage

Whilst on a three-month road trip around Canada, we decided to take a ferry from the town of Port Hardy at the northern tip of Vancouver Island to the port city of Prince Rupert on the mainland of British Columbia. So that I do not conjure up the wrong impression of a ferry ride, I do need to clarify that the vessel can carry more than 100 vehicles and 600 people. It has gift shops, dining services, and cabins. The voyage is approximately 500 miles long, taking approximately 20 hours. Although not the same level of luxury as a cruise, it is certainly not your standard harbour ferry crossing.

Whilst we did not go as far north as the USA state of Alaska, stopping instead near the most northernmost tip of mainland Canada, we did venture up the glacial fjords of the famous Inland Passage. The trip sails between the mainland and the many islands just off the coast—effectively a network of passages where the land on both sides is narrow and protected from the weather. With islands to the west, inlet-etched mainland to the east, the navigation of the twisting passages, is spectacularly beautiful.

Mountains rose higher. Fjords plunged deeper. Civilisation slipped away as we entered remote waters leading north through British Columbia. The captain and crew were on the lookout to give the call of a sighting. Not long after leaving Port Hardy, we managed to spot a pod of Orcas (killer whales). So special. A waterfall and even an old abandoned cannery came into view.

Sunset was after 9 p.m. with twilight until after 10 p.m. We stayed up hoping to see the full moon rising which was due at 10:30 p.m. However, with the high mountains, the time we would see the moon was effectively much later—so off to bed we went a little after 11 p.m.

Although many people slept in the aisles on the ferry, we chose to book a cabin. We were grateful to have selected the option of having a private space for the overnight sail—not only did this mean we could grab a few hours' sleep in relative comfort, but we also had somewhere to stow our luggage. The latter was of paramount importance given the length and geographical coverage of our trip. We were travelling within temperature ranges from minus 5 degrees to a high of 40 degrees Celsius. No one could say that we were travelling light.

We woke up around 4 a.m. (as dawn was breaking) and went outside to watch the world wake up. The moon was still out, creating an interesting sight amongst the light mist. It was cold outside—not surprising given we were just south of the Alaskan border. We were very happy to have dressed in thermals, beanies, gloves and down jackets. It may have been freezing cold, but it was oh so worth it.

Once again, I do not wish to downplay sailing to Alaska and experiencing wildlife, such as polar bears, up close. But our ferry trip up the Inland Passage was spectacular and memorable—and we got to see Orcas—at a fraction of the cost of a cruise and without spending extra days on the water.

The second example of an undertaking that is closely akin to the Alaskan Cruise and arguably equally spectacular is in the Southern Hemisphere.

Navigating the Icebergs of Antarctica

The cruise company, Azamara, had just introduced a new ship into its fleet and with the latest vessel, a new set of itineraries. One of these included sailing to Antarctica from Buenos Aires. Having wanted to return to the *Paris of South America* ever since an earlier sojourn and liking the idea of visiting Antarctica, when the opportunity presented itself, we could not resist.

After a few days spent in Buenos Aires recovering from jetlag and exploring the vibrant city, we embarked on the ship. The large vessel departed on a late-night journey for a day in Montevideo, Uruguay before the long sail down the coast to Ushuaia—nicknamed the "End of the World" and the southernmost point in South America. Leaving Ushuaia, we were unsure what to expect as crossing the Drake Passage is notoriously rough. Much as we were told that there was a five-metre swell, we seemed to be rolling over it, so it was more comfortable than expected. We could not have wished for better conditions when crossing the treacherous body of water between South America's Cape Horn, Chile and the South Shetland Islands of Antarctica.

We spent three incredible days cruising the breathtaking Antarctic Sound, drifting through a world of brilliant blue icebergs, penguin rookeries, and whales breaching the icy waters. An absolutely pristine part of God's creation, seemingly untouched by human hands. The hundreds of icebergs come in all sorts of shapes and sizes and in a multitude of colours from white to turquoise to royal blue. The penguins seem to prefer the flatter bergs—and we ooh-ed and aah-ed as we watched them sliding into the water, swimming around, and jumping back out. And then repeating this manoeuvre over and over again.

We visited Deception Island, an island in the South Shetland Islands archipelago with one of the safest harbours in Antarctica. The island is the caldera of an active volcano that seriously damaged local scientific stations when it erupted in 1967 and 1969. It previously held a whaling station but is now a tourist destination and scientific base, containing Argentine and Spanish research stations.

A startling, key destination was Iceberg Alley. This is where the bulk of the icebergs floating in the Southern Ocean come from. On the way to the alley, we passed a HUGE iceberg. When this berg broke off on 25 February 2018, it was 40-50 km long. A year later it was still sizable, measuring over 20 km. Looking at the gigantic expanse of ice, it is hard to imagine that 90% of it is hidden from view underwater. As we neared Iceberg Alley, we dressed up in all our layers and ventured outside, soon gaining an understanding of where the alley got its name. A long expanse of ice and bergs floating all over the place. We were unable to remain in the area as long as the captain had hoped as the wind had picked up and he needed to move quickly to avoid the ship being boxed in or positioned on a collision course with an iceberg.

We followed the flow of icebergs, reaching more open, rough seas. The swell meant that our run on the treadmill that afternoon was somewhat challenging as the ship rocked and rolled from side to side.

As we approached Elephant Island in the grey mist, we had some sense of what it must have felt like when Shackleton and his men were there. As we rounded the northeast corner to Wild Point, we caught a glimpse of the beach where his men made camp and where today there is a statue commemorating his expedition.

Our trip back across the Drake Passage was far less comfortable than we had experienced going down, but still not nearly as bad as expected. We woke to the ship healing over to the port side due to the strong winds, with our stateroom much closer to the water. Soon thereafter, we changed direction and now the wind was blowing directly towards our stateroom. The wind was howling and we could feel the cold air streaming into the room through the less than air-tight doorway. The entire day and following night our room was freezing—cranking the heating up to over 25 degrees had little effect. It was good to get through the winds and to have the ship sailing flat again.

Admiring Icebergs and Orcas

I feel perfectly content at having seen the Orcas breaching in the Inside Passage and being awed by giant icebergs in Antarctica. I do not think I am going to feel the need to brave the cold weather again any time soon. I shall leave that to one or more of my readers.

Are you going to take up the challenge? Are you already searching for a cruise to take you check out the icebergs and polar bears?

Summary

Some experiences that may be deemed comparable to a big-ticket item are significant in their own right. They may be well-known but do not form part of the finite list, the "Top 20." Others may not be as significant or well-known. I have made peace with many of the big-ticket things that I have almost done, in some instances even thinking that my experience was far better than the "original." One day, I may get to do the "real thing," but it is not important to me right now. I am grateful to have been able to experience these things. Although they may not have the bragging rights of the more well-known or bigger items, they are special because they are different and I have done them. Reflecting on the "almost done" items gave me a great deal of satisfaction and reduced the list of "Top 20" items that were still outstanding.

POINTS FOR REFLECTION

Look back at the list of the "Top 20" in Chapter 3 and identify if there are any items that you could say you have completed in some capacity or have done a variation.

Celebrate them!

Decide whether you are happy with that experience or whether you have unfinished business. Where there is unfinished business, what are you going to do about it?

6

Up for Grabs

Given I was using the finite "Top 20" list as my yardstick, for the sake of completeness, there are a number of items that I have not done at all that I need to address. There are those that I do not feel are in line with my passion and so I have chosen to remove from my consideration, not allowing them to use up valuable brain space. Then there are those that I am still interested in doing, those that I could call unrealised dreams. I am not going to be tempted to say that they are on a list of things to do before I die, a *bucket list*. But suffice it to say, I still have some interest in walking the Great Wall of China, skydiving and seeing my favourite band.

Walk the Great Wall of China

Over time, this endeavour has become something I have thought that I would like to do. I am not sure if it is because I have a good friend who grew up in China and I feel a connection to her birthplace. Or maybe it is my increasing fascination with the history and the construction that has taken place worldwide by the different nations and in the different eras, whether it be the Incas or the Romans.

My ultimate dream would be to complete the Great Wall Marathon. Started in the late 1900s, this marathon is widely considered to be one of the world's most challenging marathons—and for good reason. The elevation is high and the course along the iconic Wall of China is arduous. Never mind that competitors have to complete the wall section twice! I convince myself that, as the brochure reads: *I will be rewarded by its breathtaking surroundings and views.* I can imagine that as I pass through the lower valley and into the villages, onlookers will be cheering and the festive atmosphere will be a real energy boost! Given I have never even been to China, this dream could be one that remains unrealised.

As I was doing a bit of additional research while writing this, I have been reminded about the Big Five Marathon in South Africa. Maybe that is another one to think about doing. Or perhaps running over the cobblestones of Rome alongside the Colosseum will become a higher priority. I resist the idea of falling for the construction of a *bucket list* but continue to feed my dreams and, as per my mother's definition, my longevity.

Skydive

Even though I have had the opportunity to take to the air in many types of flying machines—helicopters, hot air balloons, gliders, jets and seaplanes (floatplanes)—I have never jumped out of one. I have never felt the desire to do what they commonly term the *tandem jump*. This is a skydiving experience where two people jump out of an aeroplane together, strapped to one another during the entire descent. The connecting straps make it so that one person is floating above the other during the freefall, with one's back against the other's front. I recognise that I should feel safer doing it this way and hence be more enthusiastic, but for me, that does not work as a driver. Besides the fact it would seem to be far less exhilarating, I am unable to deal with the idea of being strapped to someone else, to float through the air with another body pressing on mine. What this means is that if I would like to skydive, it is going to take me a significant amount of time and money to get to the point of being allowed to jump out of the aeroplane on my own. I still have to make a call as to how important this dream is and whether to make the investment. After all, time and money spent here will take away from that spent on other things. It is all a matter of priority.

For now, I may look to do iFLY indoor skydiving. I watched Walter as an instructor took him into a wind tunnel and helped him "fly." Pretty cool at a fraction of the cost. Maybe soon this unrealised dream will move into the "Almost Dones."

See Your Favourite Band

Growing up in South Africa during the apartheid regime meant that I lived under sanctions. Penalties were imposed on the country by other nations, aimed at changing the governing structures of the land. What this led to—for people like me—was being cut off from the rest of the world. I did not see a televised Olympic Games until I emigrated to Australia in 1995, I was not allowed to hear the music from Westminster Abbey when Prince Charles (now King Charles III) married Lady Diana, and I did not taste my first McDonald's burger until the age of 32!

Apartheid sanctions also resulted in a boycott by all the famous singers and bands, so I was not exposed to visiting musicians at all. Not only did this mean I was unable to see my favourite band on stage, but the lack of awareness meant that I did not become attached to any group of performers. Living in Australia, I have attended several performances by various artists that I like. During my time in Lucca, Italy, the annual summer festival has brought numerous famous musicians to the small walled town. With the open-air performances in the piazzas, I have been able to listen to many of the well-known artists. I am currently debating whether this item should be moved to the "Almost Dones."

Summary

At the risk of subscribing to the *bucket list*, there are a few items that feature on the "Top 20" that still hold some interest for me. They were already on the radar before I embarked on the process of "measuring my life." I have ascribed some value to them. One could say that I have parked them with a view to considering what steps I take to complete them.

There are items on the "Top 20" that I have simply eliminated. They have been purged. I have chosen not to do them. This by no means implies that I do not think they are amazing experiences. I have just chosen not to give them any priority in my life and as such, not give them any air time or spend energy thinking of them. I shall enjoy other people telling me about having done them without feeling as though I too need to undertake them too. I may revisit them at some point, but for now, I am content to have decided to eliminate the following:

- See the Northern Lights
- See the Pyramids of Giza
- Drive across the country (US)
- Hike the Pacific Crest Trail
- Visit Stonehenge

Just because I have purged these items, as they are not in line with my current passions or I have deemed them to be of little personal value, does not mean that you should do the same. I encourage you to find out more about them if they pique your interest.

POINTS FOR REFLECTION

Are there any "Top 20" you would still like to do? Why?

What are you going to do about it? When?

THE FINITE LIST
WRAP UP

It was only as I described my experiences, that I truly came to terms with how fortunate I have been to do so many amazing things. Not because they happen to be on someone else's to-do list, but because each one contributed in some way to who I am. Some things just needed a decision, and others needed extensive planning and preparation, but they all took me to another place along my life's journey. I am truly grateful for each and every one.

The personal achievement I have felt is significant. At the same time, I recognise that had I not been given the chance to do these things or taken hold of the past opportunities, I may not have found the reflection process as uplifting. My lifelong drive for success has propelled me to embark on a large number of endeavours. I have also been fortunate to have the options available to do things that many others may not have.

It has been encouraging to be given kudos by others, but I do not believe having done all these things is a true measure of success or has made me better than someone else. Would I do them again given the same choice? In some instances, a resounding "YES." In others, my motivation could be called into question and my time, money and energy may have been better used elsewhere.

Would I recommend them? It depends. We all have our own journey to travel. What is important to someone else is not necessarily what is or should be important to me.

Recognising this opened up an entirely new question: *What about all the other experiences in my life—were they any less important just because others did not see them in that way and they did not appear in the "Top 20"?* This little question resulted in a big exercise; to consider everything else that I could have done or could still do. The challenge—the list of possibilities is infinite

RE-CALIBRATING YOUR COMPASS

Look at your list of "Top 20" items that are done and dusted / not quite the real deal / up for grabs.

How much of what you have chosen to do has been driven by what other people think?

Have you done things to get kudos from others? How important are other people's opinions to you in making decisions?

Knowing what you know, which ones would you do again? Which would you not do?

Which would you recommend to others? Why?

Has your awareness increased of other achievements in your life that are not on the "Top 20"? Endeavours and accomplishments that are not what others may deem to be important? How does that make you feel?

THE INFINITE LIST
THE BEST OF THE REST

Having started by using the "Top 20" as a yardstick for measuring my life, I realised that there were a considerable number of amazing things that I had done that were not included. Numerous experiences that, although they did not hit the "Top 20" list, had given me joy and inspired others to try something new.

The "Top 20" list was finite, making measurement relatively straightforward. The reflection process became a little harder as I took stock of all the other endeavours, activities and adventures throughout my life. The list of items that I have done is extensive and the possibilities of what could still be done are infinite.

Given my nature, I chose to focus on those things that seem to be riskier and more adventurous. I added the numerous items that have inspired others in the past and which I felt would likely do so in the future. Had I used other factors for selection, I could just as easily have included having a successful career, or being married for 30+ years.

Just as I had to select the items that I considered important, as you read through my tales, I challenge you to think about your own stories. I implore you not to be limited by what I have included, but to credit yourself with your own accomplishments and be looking towards what you have in mind for your life.

Think about what gives you joy and the many things that could contribute to your passions in the future. Let my stories entertain and inspire you to act on your dreams and turn them into reality.

7

Low-hanging Fruit

The items that I have included in this chapter are those that I was able to do with relatively little effort or preparation. Whilst recognising that other people may have a different perception, I consider these endeavours to be low risk and, in my case, they did not require major skills acquisition or physical preparation and training.

As you read my stories, I encourage you to think of those things that you have done that are no less significant because they did not appear on someone else's list. Those things that did not even require you to take a risk or develop a new set of skills. They merely relied on your doing rather than talking about or listing them.

Getting A Taste of the United States of America

Walter and I took a trip to the Americas in celebration of our 10th wedding anniversary. Although I had visited Chicago previously for a brief work trip, this was my first USA vacation and Walter's first experience in the third most populous country in the world (China and India are in first and second place respectively). We started the holiday in New York City (NYC). Being new to big city stays, the noise was a bit overwhelming and the accommodation we could afford was a little dingy (at that time the Australian Dollar (AUD) was worth less than half of the USD). We loved exploring the borough of Manhattan, wandering the streets of Greenwich Village, and taking the ferry first to Staten Island and then to Liberty Island, home of the Statue of Liberty. We even climbed up the inside of the great lady. One of my highlights was heading up the elevator to the top of the Empire State Building. For some reason, I did not have any desire to go up the then-intact Twin Towers. These huge structures were visible no matter where we went, and I found them a little oppressive and imposing. Little did I realise that within five months of our passing beneath them on our tour bus, they would fall in such dramatic fashion. It is sometimes difficult to comprehend that there was a time before what is commonly known as 9/11, the terrible terrorist attack on 11 September 2001.

Needing a break from our tiny hotel room and the hustle and bustle of Manhattan, we took a road trip into New York State. For our visit to Niagara Falls, we stayed on the USA side—known more for the couples from NYC that go there for a dirty weekend away than a trip to the falls. We popped over the border into Canada to view the falls from that side. We were rewarded with spectacular, expansive views of the huge body of water cascading onto the rocks below. The welcome by the Canadian border control staff was certainly friendlier than the one we received on our return to the USA! After staying on a wine estate in the Finger Lakes, and tasting some of the local Chardonnay for which they are famous, we ventured back into NYC to fly on to Los Angeles (LA).

On leaving LA Airport, we jumped in a taxi to take us to Anaheim, the home of Disneyland. The following morning, I turned into a child again! Hearing the music of "It's a Small World," hugging Mickey and Minnie Mouse, and going on all the rides was a thrill. As we were staying just across the road from the theme park, we lived and breathed the wonders of Disneyland and its neighbouring park, California Dreaming, for the next three days. That is, apart from a day trip to Universal Studios—it was Walter's birthday and that was his choice as a birthday gift. When he expressed the desire to go to Universal Studios for his birthday, he must have known that he would get to have a tea party with "Lucy" of "I Love Lucy" fame—not the original character but the current, dressed-up version. At that time, *Shrek* was in production and we were shown how they went about creating the big green ogre and his donkey friend.

This trip was only a taste of the USA, and I always assumed I would go back, but have not done so yet. At this point, I do not have a desire to do so. I have parked a return visit for now.

Is there a location/country that you have always wanted to visit? If you have been, did it live up to your expectations? If not, why?

What is the best holiday that you can remember taking? What made it so memorable? If you took the same trip now, do you think it would be equally noteworthy or is now the time to try something different?

Sampling Argentina, Chile and Brazil

On a trip to explore South America, we chose to take in some of the big cities of South America, namely Rio de Janeiro, Buenos Aires, and Santiago. Brazil's well-known city of Rio de Janeiro was as spectacular as expected. Sugarloaf Mountain was truly as stunning as in the pictures—both to look at from below and providing a magnificent view of the city and ocean from the top that we reached via cable car. The stretch of white sand along the famous Copacabana and Ipanema beaches went on for miles. Or to be more precise, approximately 20 kilometres. The reason I can remember this detail is that we ran on the beachfront from our hotel in Ipanema to Copacabana and back.

The amazing thing was that we were able to run in the middle of the wide two-lane road that follows this long expanse of beach. Every Sunday and public holiday, the road is closed to traffic and taken over by the public as they run, cycle, rollerblade, and walk. With everyone exercising like that, it is little wonder that Brazilians have such great bodies and can wear the swimwear they do!

Walking along the beachfront during the day felt perfectly safe, but when we ventured a couple of streets back, we felt more vulnerable and needed to keep our wits about us to avoid pickpockets and other dodgier characters.

We found Rio to be the most difficult of the South American cities to navigate, mainly due to language. Brazil is the continent's only Portuguese-speaking nation, with all the other countries communicating in Spanish. In South America, English is not spoken as widely as it is in Europe, but we did find it more prevalent in Spanish-speaking countries. I found Portuguese to be a much harder language to understand and my French expertise did not help me as much as it did with Spanish.

A side trip from Rio to Buzios, a seaside village frequented in the 1960s by Brigitte Bardot, was worth the two-hour trip on a local bus. I can understand why the famous French actress chose the beautiful tiny village with its pristine white beaches to hide out with her then-Brazilian boyfriend. During the time on the bus, we had no idea where we were, where we were going, or where to get off. There were no other tourists on the bus and the instructions were in Portuguese. This was before smartphones and google maps. Somehow, we made it to our destination. We stayed in a lovely *pensione* (guest house) with stunning views over the water and enjoyed many a renowned Brazilian steak at the local restaurants.

Our stay in Santiago, Chile was short but pleasant. We enjoyed a run to the top of Cerro San Cristóbal, a hill in northern Santiago, rising about 300 metres above the rest of Santiago and giving an expansive view of the city and its varied architecture. We spent one day walking amongst the vineyards followed by tasting the wines of Concha y Toro, the largest producer and exporter of wine in Latin America.

We fell in love with Buenos Aires, Argentina during our three-day stay and vowed to return. For my meat-loving husband, he had entered a land of bliss and I loved the energy of the city.

There is something edgy and unique about South America with its very distinct countries with their own culture and complexities. If you are willing to be challenged, it is worth a visit. If you are looking for a relaxing lie on the beach under palm trees, it may not be the destination for you.

Have you done something that was challenging at the time, sometimes more so than you would prefer? What did you learn about the world, other people, or about yourself?

Cruising Greece and the Greek Isles

Cruising the Greek Isles was not something I had on my radar; visiting the Greek Isles had always been my mother's dream, not mine.

It was my mother's 80th birthday. I figured that at 80, island hopping by ferry was likely to be a little challenging, particularly in the July heat. The Azamara Quest was due to sail from Athens precisely over my mother's birth date. With the cruise company priding itself on its small ships and personal service, and the itinerary designed to visit numerous islands, it seemed a perfect fit. Soon, my mother and I were flying out to Athens.

During an online search, I discovered a little apartment outside the tourist area of the city for us to stay in for a few days before we began the cruise of the islands. It was next to a garlic shop. A business that had been in the family for generations and that only sold garlic! We had to keep the bathroom window closed at all times to keep the smell out!

The apartment was in a part of the city not frequented by tourists. The people at the nearby cafes spoke little—if any—English, but the coffee and pastries were authentic and delicious. George, the guy at the local store had a big grin and I managed to get by using hand and head gestures to purchase the best cheese and produce. If we wanted bread from the bakery, we had to ensure we went early before it all sold out. On our final day, we went to a restaurant just around the corner. The owners were flabbergasted. I don't think they had ever had tourists visit their eatery before.

We wandered around the famous Plaka area, watched archaeological digs, and ate Greek yogurt with nuts and honey in one of the squares. We saw the changing of the guards in Syntagma Square, fascinated by the way they kick out with their giant shoes as they march.

A highlight of our stay in Athens was our visit to the Acropolis Museum. It is an archaeological museum focused on the findings of the site of the Acropolis of Athens and was built to house the artefacts found on the rock and the surrounding slopes. It also lies over the ruins of a part of Roman and early Byzantine Athens which can be seen underfoot through purpose-built glass floors. The museum's building was constructed with dimensions to reflect the Parthenon, the ancient temple that sits on the Acropolis, the rocky outcrop above the city of Athens. From the huge windows of the museum, the Acropolis can be seen towering over the city. As it was an extremely hot day, we appreciated being able to experience the rich history and magnificence of the structure in the air-conditioned comfort of the museum.

As a side-trip between the apartment and the ship, we went to ancient Corinth, just over an hour's drive from central Athens. There were few tourists exploring the ruins that day, so we had plenty of time and space to explore to our hearts' content. We imagined the people shopping in the *agora* and marvelled at the large Pirene Fountain—both famous in Greek mythology and as a source of water for the Apostle Paul. Before reaching ancient Corinth, we took a stop to view the Corinth Canal that connects the Ionian and Aegean Seas. I had never even dreamed about what it would look like, and even then, I was taken aback. How the huge ships manoeuvre through that narrow passage of water begs belief. On occasions, the canal has been blocked as a result of a series of landslides. When the waterway remains closed for an extended period of time, preventing vessels from using this significant thoroughfare, it has a huge impact on shipping in the region. Fortunately, the canal was open whilst we were there and we watched a huge vessel making its way down the narrow channel of water.

On the way to the Greek Islands, the cruise went via Kusadasi, Turkey, where we had the opportunity to take a tour of Ancient Ephesus. Even though it was chaotic and hot, my mother was in her element, walking where the Apostle Paul had walked while he spread the good news about Jesus. By the time we arrived back at the ship, she was exhausted—but happy.

The ancient walled structures on the Greek islands of Kos and Rhodes were visible from our balcony of the ship, allowing my mother to sit and savour the view while I went ashore and explored every nook and cranny that I could in the short time allowed by the port call. I was not much of a history lover at school, but spending time in ancient cities and ruins allows me to dream and to do my utmost to visualise what life was like in days gone by. And in many instances, to appreciate how comfortable most of us have it today.

One afternoon on Kos, following a run along the beachfront promenade, I found myself stranded ashore. To allow another vessel into the harbour, the captain was required to move the ship a few metres, which meant lifting gangplanks and removing all lines. Fortunately, the weather was warm and I could stand by enjoying the spectacle. Once the ship had moved the required distance, the gangway was put in place and I was able to board.

The pure white and blue buildings of Santorini looked exactly as they do on postcards!

The final stop was on the mainland. In the town of Nafplion—originally Greek's capital – I climbed to the Palamidi fortress, nestled on the crest of a 216-metre-high hill above the town. It was worth every one of the more than 900 steps to explore the eight bastions and the spectacular view.

Whilst Greece had not been one of my target destinations, my time there had whetted my appetite for the history, scenery, and people. A few years later, at the end of a cruise from Venice to Athens to celebrate our 25th wedding anniversary, I was happy to be able to "show" Walter both Nafplion (including the views from the fortress) and guide him on a fleeting 24-hour pass through Athens.

We would like to go back and explore the area in more detail. I am resisting saying "It's on my *bucket list*" and if it were, I have not yet determined where it would sit in terms of priority. Maybe it is still in the dream category and will not ever be converted into a passionate pursuit. What I do know is that my mother's dream turned out to have an impact on my own dreams and desires.

Is there something you have done for someone else where you had little or no interest in doing it? How did it make you feel to help make someone else's dreams come true? Did the experience ignite a desire in you to do it again or perhaps to do even more?

Circumnavigating the Baltic Sea

I had certainly never thought of visiting the Baltic Sea and to this day, I am still a little unsure of how I ended up going there. Perhaps I felt guilty that I had left my husband at home to take my mother cruising. Perhaps I was less concerned with *where* I was going than *how* I was going and wanted another experience of the luxury and grandeur that I had enjoyed on the Azamara Quest. Notwithstanding, a few years after the Greece trip, Walter and I set off on a flight to Stockholm—this time to hop on to the Azamara Quest's sister ship, the Azamara Journey.

We arrived in Stockholm at the end of June—midsummer. The longest day of the year is celebrated at this time, and this far north, the longest day of the year is one where the sun never sets. The sun appears to go down and start coming up almost simultaneously.

A new museum had opened in Stockholm just before our visit. ABBA The Museum is a Swedish interactive exhibition about the pop band ABBA, showcasing their collected works in a contemporary, interactive setting. It was fun to revisit my growing years, singing "Fernando" at the top of my voice into a microphone and dancing in front of a green screen. Not the most impressive or educational venue ever visited, but unusual and entertaining. It was a good way to spend a few hours in between our arrival and embarking the ship.

The ship was docked in the port of Stockholm for our first night so we had extra time to explore the city. During the walking tour around *Gamla Stan*, the old town of Stockholm, I stopped to stand in Borgargården square, looking up at the giant façade of the City Hall. This magnificent building is famous for its grand ceremonial halls and unique pieces of art and is the venue of the Nobel Prize banquet held on 10 December every year to celebrate the awarding of the peace prize. On top of the old Parliament building, the Rooftop Walking Tour along a catwalk 43 metres above the ground overlooking Stockholm's famed Gamla Stan, or Old Town, gave us a bird's eye view of the city.

The benefit of travelling around the Baltic Sea by ship became increasingly evident as we docked at different ports in various countries. With most not being part of the European Union (EU), currencies used varied between countries and languages were equally diverse. Within the safety of our floating hotel, it was easy for us to arrive in a new port and country each morning without having to think about studying the dictionary or changing money. With everything catered for on board, we did not need to spend money or organise activities ashore.

The Helsinki Cathedral, a magnificent white building arising from the top of a giant staircase was impressive, but the Temppeliaukio Church, also known as "Church in the Rock," was unique and far more memorable. This church, built in the late 1060s is carved into the rock and has a stunning copper dome. After a day of sightseeing, the cool serenity of entering into the building cut into the hillside was very welcome. It was peaceful and we took time to sit on the wooden pews to enjoy the ambience.

We docked in Kiel, Germany, during the world-renowned tall ships festival, and were able to wander along the piers admiring the enormous wooden vessels. Being a lover of Weissbier (wheat beer), Walter was eager to enjoy a drink (or two) in its "home country." Even though he wasn't feeling well at the time (he had caught a bit of a cold), he could not resist sitting down at one of the festival bars along the water to enjoy his favourite drink, the top-fermented beer which is brewed with a large proportion of wheat relative to the amount of malted barley. A highlight was standing on the foredeck of our cruise ship watching the fireworks that bring the festival to an end.

All parts of the world have their own beauty, things that make them worth visiting, but what really sets each place apart are its people. We only spent a day in Copenhagen, Denmark (so are in no position to have an opinion on the nature of the general public), but what did stand out for us above all (pun intended) was how tall everyone was. Similarly, in Tallinn Estonia, we were astounded at the number of beautiful, blonde women and girls, like characters from a fairytale.

St Petersburg, Russia, was a highlight of the voyage, and would certainly have been much more challenging on our own—due to the restrictions on free movement for tourists. We still had to pass through passport control every time we embarked and disembarked, but otherwise, as long as we were with a tour guide, we were able to move away from the ship. With the strict rules in the country, it would have been difficult or nigh on impossible to obtain visas to be able to enable us to travel independently, even though that is typically our preferred option. The one downside about having a guide every time we left the ship—even the night we were treated to a Russian Ballet—was that we were subjected to tourist commentary on the bus back to the ship. Particularly after having had a relaxing night out at the theatre, I would have preferred a quiet bus journey.

Since our visit, I now have a friend with Estonian heritage and whilst she lives between Florence, Italy and Brussels, Belgium, our friendship has further piqued my interest in her home country; so often it comes down to the people.

Maybe I have whetted your appetite to consider visiting one or more of the destinations around the Baltic. Or possibly you have heard enough to satisfy your curiosity. Perhaps it has triggered a desire in you to attend the ballet or take a rooftop walk in a city. It could be that you haven't tried

Weissbier before and would like to do so. (That you can likely do close to home—your choice.)

Is there something you have thought about doing and cannot put your finger on why? Has the "why" factor stopped you from doing it? Or is the "how" that has stopped you. If it seems overwhelming, is there an easier way for you to have a similar experience?

Watching Ballet at the Vienna Opera House

During an extended stay in Florence, Italy, we took a short trip to Austria to take in the sights of Vienna and check out the Danube River. My husband surprised me with tickets to a ballet at the Vienna Opera House. Having grown up as a dancer and going to the ballet on numerous occasions with my mother and grandmother, he knew this would be a treat. Fortunately, he had the foresight to book well in advance of our trip—not only did we have near-perfect seats, but the performance was booked out. We thoroughly enjoyed getting dressed up for the occasion—I wore a long dress and Walter was in his suit— and it was good to see that those around us had done the same. Not only was it amazing to go to a ballet for the first time in years and to go inside this magnificent building, but it was also staggering that Walter had agreed to watch a ballet. I think his experiences of Russian ballet in St Petersburg followed by ballet in the Vienna Opera House have spoilt him and it is likely to be hard to convince him to do it again in a lesser venue. I think he has certainly ticked that off his list. I am not sure about me.

Do you have a childhood activity that you have given up for some reason? Something you are still interested in? Does that prompt a desire in you to relive it in some way—big or small?

Marvelling at the Lipizzaners at the Spanish Riding School

Whilst on the same trip to Vienna, another once-in-a-lifetime opportunity presented itself. Unlike the ballet, this one was unplanned. During our stay in Vienna, the white Lipizzaner horses were appearing with the equally renowned Vienna Boys Choir. Sadly, all performances were sold out, but we were able to attend one of the two-hour training sessions and watch the beautiful stallions go through their paces.

Prior to our visit, I had no idea that all the Lipizzaners are born dark and they lighten over time to turn into the white stallions we typically see. That said, the school always houses a black stallion, which is meant to bring good luck. Such animals are said to be only one in a thousand of the Lippazan population.

My horse-mad niece, Courtney, would surely have had a visit to the home of the Lipizzaner on her *bucket list*. For me, it was something I knew about but had never thought much about. I sent her photos and bought her memorabilia in the hope that she could enjoy some of the experience vicariously through me. Sometimes it almost does not seem fair when someone else gets to do something we are passionate about and we don't.

Have you ever missed out on doing something that you were passionate about when someone else you know did it? How did it make you feel?

Have you ever done something that you are aware someone else would be desperate to do? How can you make them appreciate the experience vicariously through you?

Experiencing the Fundy Tides

The Bay of Fundy is a bay between the Canadian provinces of New Brunswick and Nova Scotia, with a small portion touching the USA state of Maine. It has the highest tidal range in the world. Twice a day, the Bay of Fundy is filled and emptied of a billion tons of water – more than the flow of all the world's freshwater rivers.

After visiting family members in Florenceville, we drove southwest across the province of New Brunswick, hitting the coast at the Fundy National Park and the village of Alma. Whilst we had heard and read about the tidal variations, nothing had prepared us for what we would see. Having sailed in The Whitsundays off the coast of Australia, we had experienced changes in tides of a few metres, where boat keels hit the ocean floor when people misjudge their anchoring and wide beaches are exposed by the outgoing tide. But nowhere have we seen anything near the more than fifteen-metre change we witnessed in the Bay of Fundy!

We reached Alma at close to low tide, so all the fishing boats were on dry land, most resting on boxes to protect the bottom of the vessels. We were only able to truly understand the extent of this tidal phenomenon when we visited at high tide the following day and the "dry docks" were full of water and most of the boats had gone out fishing–probably for lobsters.

Further north along the Bay of Fundy are the Hopewell Rocks— known as *sea stacks*, the rock formations are caused by tidal erosion. You can walk around the famous "flowerpot rocks" at low tide and then watch them disappear as the tide rises. We were fortunate to be staying at a bed and breakfast a kilometre away from the rocks, so visited the rocks at various stages within the tide cycle. Unfortunately, the winds were extremely strong whilst we were there and created a huge swell, so our kayaking trip around the rocks at high tide was cancelled. However, we did experience the rising of the tide from the beach surrounding the Hopewell Rocks, and I was the last person to leave the sand except for the staff from Parks Canada. It was incredible to watch how quickly the water level rose and eventually swallowed up the beach that we had been standing on minutes before.

From Hopewell Rocks, we made our way into Nova Scotia to visit relatives in Truro before heading down to explore the southern coast. What we hadn't realised was that our Fundy tide experience was to continue.

We visited the Fundy Tidal Interpretive Centre where we stood on the observation deck and watched the flow of the Shubenacadie River reverse in front of our eyes as the water emptied from the Bay of Fundy (what began as a flat river turned into a mass of waves and eddies). An hour later, further upriver and just outside Truro, we stood gob-smacked as the wave of the tidal bore approached, almost swallowing up the river as it went. When the tidal bore approaches, completely drained riverbeds are filled. Over the years, the sudden influx of water has claimed the lives of several tourists who were in the dry riverbeds when the bore came rushing in.

There are approximately 60 tidal bores in the world. Prior to my experience in Canada, the only one that I had heard of and seen on television was the one on the Amazon River. Called the Pororoca, this tidal bore occurs in the estuary, before spring tides. Perhaps, unlike me, you are an expert on tidal bores and have travelled the world looking for them. If you are a surfer, you may even have tackled the waves on your board. As someone new to this phenomenon, I found the bore fascinating; but I was more enthralled by the enormous Fundy tide changes where the river connected with the sea. I do not plan on seeking out any other tidal bores, but this experience piqued my interest such that I would check out another one if I were in the vicinity.

The tidal bore is an amazing natural phenomenon that I knew very little about. Have you stumbled across something amazing while out doing something else? Has that increased your interest to the point of seeking out more?

Exploring the Eastern Side of Canada

The visit to the Bay of Fundy was part of a bigger experience. When most tourists from Australia consider travelling to Canada, they immediately think of British Columbia—Vancouver for nightlife, Whistler for skiing, and perhaps Vancouver Island for outdoor activities. Then their minds may go to Alberta, including Banff, Jasper, and Lake Louise for hiking the Canadian Rocky Mountains or to view those bright turquoise lakes. Unfortunately, in the large majority of cases, people have limited time and with Canada being enormous, there is insufficient opportunity to cover the rest of the country.

We were fortunate to have three months to explore the vast country, so we split our time and territory in half. The first six weeks were spent covering the typical itinerary described above: hiking, walking on glaciers, flying in floatplanes—and building a snowman, not only for the very first time but in weather that was considered mid-summer. The remaining six weeks of my time in the country were spent in what could be termed the eastern side (which included the Bay of Fundy).

With Canada being such a vast country—it even swallows up the continent of Australia—we chose to fly from west to east, boarding the plane in Vancouver for the five-hour flight to Ottawa. We stayed with friends who had been born and grew up in the nation's capital, enabling us to experience the city from the perspective of a local. We spent hours on borrowed bicycles, cycling along the Rideau Canal into the city and surrounds. At 35 degrees celsius, it was hard to imagine that in winter the temperature would drop to -35C and that the canal would be frozen, enabling city workers to ice skate to the office.

The changing of the guards at Parliament Hill is a popular tourist activity. As with most of our Ottawa experience, the insider view provided us with a day that we will not forget. We went to the Cartier Square Drill Hall where the parade begins. Here we chatted to Brian the drum major—he had relinquished his baton to his understudy for the day but couldn't stay away! Walking alongside the guards to the parliament grounds was great fun, even in the extreme heat.

We frequented the expansive Parliament surrounds a few more times during our stay, most memorably on 1 July, which is Canada Day. The highlight of the festivities was the air show by the Snowbirds. We arrived at "The Hill" just in time to see the first aircraft buzz overhead. Officially known as the Canadian Forces 431 Air Demonstration Squadron, the Snowbirds are Canada's military aerobatic air show flight demonstration team whose purpose is to "demonstrate the skill, professionalism, and teamwork of Canadian Forces personnel." And boy were they skilled! We could not believe how close they flew to each other while in formation.

Nova Scotia is ruggedly spectacular, Montreal cosmopolitan and very French, and the historic district of Quebec City is quaint and European in feel and architecture. Cape Breton was remote with beautiful forests, green landscapes and sea vistas and Toronto was a vibrant, busy city. Prince Edward Island (PEI), famous for potatoes and lobsters, is also the setting for Anne of Green Gables, a novel by Canadian author Lucy Maud Montgomery. As I write this, I am tempted to start writing a book on Canada, particularly about what appears to be the lesser-known, underappreciated "east side." I fear that by trying to pull out a few highlights, I have been unable to do it justice. The east side of Canada is worth a visit; it has everything to keep adventure seekers, foodies and boaties amused—and historians fascinated.

Have you been somewhere or done something that few people in your circle of friends or family know about? Did they show little interest or give you no kudos? If so, did that make you feel that the experience was any less valuable?

Relaxing in Zanzibar

I ended up in Zanzibar simply because it was in Tanzania and near Mount Kilimanjaro. I had always thought I would like to visit Morocco, the land of spice and colour and this small island seemed to me to have similar characteristics. Add to that the long white beaches and gleaming blue ocean, I could not resist spending a few days in Zanzibar to recover after the challenging climb to the mountain summit.

Zanzibar is an autonomous region of Tanzania. It is composed of the Zanzibar Archipelago in the Indian Ocean, 25–50 kilometres off the coast of the mainland, and consists of many small islands and two large ones: Unguja (the main island, referred to informally as Zanzibar) and Pemba Island. The capital is Zanzibar City, located on the island of Unguja. Its historic centre is Stone Town, a World Heritage Site.

Stone Town is a feast for the senses. With its regular calls to prayer sounding over loudspeakers placed throughout the town, there is limited opportunity for silence, even in the middle of the night. We stayed in a room that had a rooftop bathroom (no walls) which offered little way of escaping the calls booming through the loudspeakers – we could reduce it by closing the door leading up the stairway from the bedroom. I loved walking the streets, sampling the coffee in the quaint coffee shops and admiring the art and artefacts in the shops. The fresh food market was busy and smelly—and the meat and chicken were covered in flies! But it was a welcome break to sit at a bar sipping a cocktail whilst watching the beautifully carved *dhows* (wooden boats) sail by as the sun set across the ocean.

After a few nights in Stone Town, we escaped the buzz to one of the beach resorts for a treat—a huge villa with a private plunge pool and direct access to the white sandy beach. A good way to wind down after the strenuous mountain climb to the top of Mount Kilimanjaro; although we felt more like tourists and less like visitors absorbing the culture.

I would still like to visit Morocco, but if I never get there, I do feel satisfied. I am grateful to have uncovered this little gem called Zanzibar.

Have you stumbled across a little gem of a location? What did you particularly enjoy or were surprised by?

Living in a Cave in Matera

Matera, one of the oldest cities in the world, is situated on a rocky outcrop in the region of Basilicata, in southern Italy. From the Neolithic age until today, human activity has taken place on this site without interruption. It is home to cave dwellings called the "Sassi" (stones) and was declared a UNESCO World Heritage site in 1993. In this city, contrasts reign supreme, with the tangle of cave houses, Baroque buildings, and stunning churches reflecting the tumultuous past.

The city spans two natural amphitheatres—the Sasso (stone) Caveoso and Sasso Barisano. Underneath the warren of above-ground buildings, there is an underground city of tunnels, cisterns to collect water, and churches built into the rock. At sunset, the city transforms into a giant nativity scene.

The biblical landscapes and lovely natural surroundings have attracted filmmakers, resulting in films like the "Passion of Christ" and "Ben Hur" being shot in Matera. The Bond movie, "No Time to Die" made the most of the rocky outcrops and monochrome nature of the small town.

Unfortunately, life in Matera was not always so glamorous. Whilst it began as a place where clergy and aristocracy filled the streets, there was a period in Matera's history where it was regarded as the "shame of Italy." Even people like Olivetti (the typewriter guy) played a part in trying to bring it out of ruin when in the mid-1900s, he raised awareness of the conditions in which people were living and the residents were relocated to newly built housing outside the Sassi. This left an empty shell that was left abandoned until the 1990s.

The cave we stayed in is a part of this history, part of a cave complex called Corte San Pietro. The husband-and-wife team who run the complex have been renovating the compact property of five cave rooms and dining room around a courtyard since 1990, installing plumbing, electricity, heating, and ventilation systems to counter the subterranean humidity. "My wife's family was violently against us living here," Fernando told us. "Back then, the Sassi had been abandoned, virtually given over to wolves." While working on their caves—which gives new meaning to the term "fixer-upper"—they discovered eight interconnected cisterns below the floor, part of a network developed to catch rainwater for drinking. "We had no idea these were here until we started," he said. "They had been filled with debris." The cisterns are now being turned into a "soul spa" for meditation.

Near the hotel was a reproduction of a cave house as it would have been in the slum days – although this time it was clean. It is hard for me to imagine that a family of up to 10 people and livestock (pigs, chickens and horses) would have shared the space. Children would have shared the bed with their parents and slept on top of tables and chests (maybe with mattresses laid on top).

Have you done something fun but been confronted by the reality of the situation? Have you enjoyed it, found it educational or wished you had not been there at all?

Summary

I realise that I have taken for granted some of the amazing experiences I have had in my life. I recognise that I have been presented with a number of opportunities that many others would not. Just because something is not on the "Top 20" list, and is relatively unknown, or does not seem to require a lot of effort on our part does not lessen its significance. What feels as though it "just happened" to one person could feel like a huge undertaking to another.

I hope that in reading this chapter you have realised the significance of some of the things you have done or events that have taken place in your life. As you have taken advantage of the opportunities around you, you may have done things that many others may only dream about or not even be aware of.

POINTS FOR REFLECTION

Are there incredible things that you have done or experienced in your life that feel as though they have "just happened"?

Why do you consider them incredible?

How did they contribute to who and where you are today?

Taking Chances

When thinking through the events of my life, I realise that I have embarked on endeavours that many people may feel a bit nervous about, as the physical risk was higher than what someone would typically experience while sightseeing. Whilst not necessarily needing high-level expertise, some activities required a certain skill level beyond what could be deemed standard or there was an amount of time and effort involved in preparing to undertake the pursuit.

Flying a Plane

I have frequently said that I would love to have been a pilot, but with imperfect sight—I have worn glasses since the age of two—I probably would not be accepted as a commercial aviator. The first time I remember being a passenger in a plane was for a scenic trip in a small aircraft over Victoria Falls in what was then Rhodesia (now Zimbabwe) at the age of seven. I went with my dad and two brothers— my mother, unlike me, is scared of heights, so did not join us. Several years later, I came closer to being in the role of pilot when I took a commercial flight for work. This was on another small plane—so small that I had to climb up on the wing and sit in the co-pilot's seat. I can still picture coming in to land at the airport in Johannesburg— approaching the runway at night and seeing the bright lights flash before me.

I am not sure if it is despite or because of these opportunities, that I still had a yearning to fly a plane myself. When Walter surprised me with a half-day private introductory course at Bankstown Airport in Sydney, I was ecstatic. After some time in the classroom, the instructor took me out to the little Cessna to complete the pre-flight checks. I had trouble seeing over the dashboard as the instructor had forgotten his cushion, but that did not stop me from taking the controls, navigating down the runway (a little side to side as I became used to the foot control) and pulling us up into the air. The half-hour flight was over much too quickly, and soon I was landing the little bird on the ground and taxiing back (a little straighter this time).

Another opportunity for me to take the controls came about when we joined friends to go for a spin in their two-seater motorised glider. Bob hopped into the cockpit ready to get going, only to find that the aircraft battery was flat. Fortunately, we had jumper cables for our car, so soon we had them hooked up between the plane and his 4WD. The aeroplane battery was soon charged, and we were ready to get on our way. After using the engine to lift us into the air, Bob turned it off. Soaring in the silence over the Southern Highlands south of Sydney was dreamlike and I was sad that we eventually had to land. I never thought I would be flying in a plane that had to be jumpstarted!

Whilst I have had limited time behind the controls, I am grateful that I have had the opportunity to do so. My ideal would still be to qualify as a pilot, but I am happy that I have been able to enjoy these varied experiences. If I have another opportunity to fly a plane,

I will definitely take it, but I am satisfied, and content with what I have done.

Do you have something you have always wanted to do, have done once or twice, but somehow feel as though you would like to do more? What if you never do so again? Can you be content with what you've experienced?

Soaring in a Hot Air Balloon

I do not remember the precise moment at which I saw my first hot air balloon or what made me decide that going up in one was something I wanted to do. I do recall the chilly Easter morning in Canberra, Australia when I woke early to go running and saw hundreds of balloons of all shapes and sizes taking off into the clear blue skies for the Canberra Balloon Festival. One of them was in the shape of a Scottish bagpipe player! Maybe this was when my desire was triggered. Or perhaps it was when friends told me about their experience floating across the skies. They also shared how frequently they had booked a flight and had it cancelled due to unfavourable weather. It was the latter, together with the cost, that put me off booking a flight and taking the long drive typically required to arrive at the take-off spot.

But when friends in Sydney told us they had booked a balloon for the morning and invited us to join their family for the trip, I certainly was not going to say *No*. Concern set in the day before as a change in weather moved in. Even as we took the more than one-hour drive into the countryside to the take-off location, there was some uncertainty as to whether the flight would get off the ground. When we eventually took off over the misty valley, I was relieved and excited. When the pilot switched off the gas, there was nothing but silence as we floated above the countryside. We felt as though we were suspended in mid-air with nothing to hold us.

The scenery over the outer suburbs of Sydney was pretty, but one day I would like to join the hundreds of other balloons soaring over Cappadocia in Turkey, regarded as the most famous hot air balloon experience. It is a vision, a dream, an idea. I have not planned it yet. Will I choose to make the effort, or will it remain a dream? Time will tell. At this stage, I am comfortable with that ambiguity. It is not a core passion, so can wait. And perhaps it will never happen. That is okay too.

Is there something you have dreamed of doing, or have done, but would like to do differently? How much effort have you put into making it happen? If you have not done so, perhaps it is not important enough and you can let it go—at least for now.

Sailing Turkey's Turquoise Coast

Turkey is a destination that was never on my radar. Geographically, it was far away and I was not aware of having ever met someone from the region. Yet, I ended up spending two weeks on a yacht sailing around the beautiful bays on what is known as the Turquoise Coast. It is not hard to see why it is called that. The water is a dreamy shade of blue and the enormous cliffs that appear to rise from the water add to the dramatic scenery.

The trip to Turkey came about as a result of compounding events. Walter and I had not sailed before, but after a two-day course, we headed off to the Whitsunday Islands in Queensland, Australia to try our hands at a week of bareboating. (Bareboating is the act of chartering a sailboat that one lives upon, navigates, and operates for a vacation from an owner or a charter company.) We so enjoyed our vacation, living on the chartered sailboat, and navigating it around the islands that soon afterwards we bought a 36-foot Jeanneau yacht. As sailing was not our main sport, and for the income and tax benefits it involved, the yacht was put into charter in the Whitsundays through a company called Sunsail. The arrangement with Sunsail allowed us to use our own boat, Genesis, a certain number of weeks a year. The added advantage was that we could also charter a similar vessel at any of their bases in the world at no cost for a couple of weeks each year. When we looked for somewhere to go for a two-week holiday, we checked out our sailing options and chose Gocek, Turkey.

We arrived in Istanbul early one morning with a day to occupy before flying to Dalaman near the coast. Nothing had prepared me for the vibrant, chaotic sounds and smells of the Grand Bazaar and the pushy carpet salesmen on every corner. For a young woman with a sheltered upbringing in South Africa, it was a little overwhelming. Even so, we had a fun day checking out the Blue Mosque and seeing where Asia meets Europe over the Bosphorus River.

Our arrival at Dalaman airport that afternoon was no less dramatic. We did not know that there were two terminals, one international, and one domestic. We had arrived at the domestic and had no idea where we were supposed to meet the person who was to take us to the Sunsail base to board the chartered vessel. Despite our desperate attempts, we were unable to find anyone that spoke English, but after a few quick runs back and forth between the two terminals, we eventually found our driver and we were on our way. We thought the excitement was over, but the drive to the base in Göcek was full of drama—I did not know that four cars could fit side by side on a two-lane road! But somehow, the vehicles moved around each other as they came around the bends on the mountainous road and crashes were avoided. We made it! When we finally arrived, we were happy to find that one of the Sunsail staff was an Aussie—and whilst we did not know him personally, he gave us a touch of familiarity.

The next morning, I woke up with my eye totally swollen – I was unable to open it or see a thing. There were spiders in the area, so it could have been a spider bite. A bit scary when in a strange land and far away from civilisation—let alone doctors. Thankfully, within 24 hours, the swelling had gone down and all was well on board. We could be on our merry way without having to find a vehicle or vessel to take us further afield to locate a doctor.

The sailing was easy. We were always in line of sight of land and the waters were sheltered as they were largely within bays. Generally, each little bay had a place for mooring and a family-run restaurant. The restaurant was typically part of the family home where guests sat at tables out in the open.

There was not much water between the keel and the sea bottom in many of the bays and marinas along our journey so we found it better not to look at the navigation charts, but rather to rely on local experts to guide us as we approached our chosen bay for the night and reversed into our little spot next to other boats moored in the various bays and marinas. This mooring method is termed *Med Mooring*—a method of getting as many boats into as small an area as possible. The Mediterranean Mooring is a hybrid of anchoring, rafting, and docking and is used in regions where there is little room to dock and minimum tidal range. It takes its name from an old Mediterranean custom of mooring stern-to (backside first) along a town's quay or sea wall, a system that allows a large number of boats to fit in a small place. I became an expert at reversing the vessel and Walter was very proficient in running around the boat, tying ropes, and throwing others to the adults and children that were helping us tie up.

One of my favourite mooring locations was on a dilapidated wooden pier in the bay that housed Redchup's boat. Redchup was a local restaurateur living on an old unseaworthy boat with his wife, mother, and two teenage children. The boat also served as a restaurant. In the waters of the bay were the ruins of what was their original brick-and-mortar home and restaurant. The building had been destroyed by the authorities as the family did not have the license required by law and the governmental controls in place had prevented them from obtaining approval.

Located about 50 kilometres from the harbour town of Fethiye, the large bay housing Redchup's boat was surrounded by pine trees and famed for the remaining ruins of Cleopatra's Baths. According to legend, Marc Anthony built a Roman Bath at this very spot for Cleopatra as a wedding gift and even had golden sand transported to this location from Egypt. This place was chosen due to the hot water spring supplied by the thermal waters of a crater lake found behind one of the mountains north of the bay. According to the myth, the queen visited here shortly after marrying Marc Anthony on what would have been their honeymoon. We were moored alongside Cleopatra's bath and could hop off the boat whenever we wanted, and swim and refresh ourselves as Cleopatra did over 2,000 years ago. It felt as if time had stood still.

Whilst sailing in turquoise waters and bathing in Cleopatra's baths is what dreams are made of, not everything could be deemed to be smooth sailing. While we were docked by these calming Roman baths, our holding tank overflowed. The holding tank contained the waste (black water) from the toilet which needed to be discharged while we were out at sea. Unfortunately, we had not emptied the holding tank before it became full. Suffice it to say, I was suitably embarrassed by the brown stuff emanating from the side of our vessel and did my utmost to distract anyone that was in the vicinity. We had to wait until we left the bay and were out in open water before we were able to rectify the situation.

Another example of this adventure not going perfectly to plan occurred near the town of Fethiye. We were on the shore, returning to the location of our anchored boat, only to spot the vessel drifting along amongst the other boats. The anchor had pulled up. We managed to reach the tender that we had tied up on the shore, rowed out, boarded the boat and reset the anchor in time to avoid any damage to our vessel or anyone else's.

Despite all the challenges, I still describe the two weeks spent sailing the Turkish coast as an amazing experience. Not only did it expand our geographic horizons, but it also exposed us to people who changed our outlook and uncovered our passion for what life would have been like in days gone by. Walking up the cliffs from our boat tied up in the little bays, we came across men walking along rocky paths with their donkeys as they would have done in biblical times and marvelled at the ruins of ancient towns.

It is only as I write this story that I am aware of how much one can experience within two weeks—the good and the less so. The trip was not all romance and champagne as many envisage a sailing trip to be. We learned a significant amount about boat handling, ourselves, each other, other people, and the world–all valuable lessons that stood us in good stead in the future and ignited a desire to continue learning and experiencing new things and meeting different people.

Had I ever thought of going to Turkey before this quick decision to take a sailing holiday there? A resounding no! Would I go back? Absolutely! Sometimes life is about taking advantage of the opportunities that present themselves and trying something new. If I had been living my life based on a list, I would have been left poorer for not having this rich experience. This trip unearthed passions in me that I had not imagined.

Do you find that you limit yourself to a list of things that you or someone else thinks you should do? Are you interested in broadening your experiences? If so, how can you go about looking for opportunities and converting them into reality?

Have you done something that you went into thinking it was going to be pure pleasure, but it turned out to be a mix of extreme highs and lows? How did it impact you?

Sailing in the Caribbean

Thanks to our investment in the yacht, one destination that I had dreamed of made it to my "done" list—the Caribbean. Whilst I had dreamed about the Caribbean, I had not identified all the island groups making up the region. I had never heard of the British Virgin Isles (BVI) until I started investigating sailing destinations.

The BVI is a British Overseas Territory in the Caribbean, east of Puerto Rico and the U.S. Virgin Islands and northwest of Anguilla. Geographically part of the Virgin Islands archipelago, the islands are located in the Leeward Islands of the Lesser Antilles and are part of the West Indies. The British Virgin Islands consist of the main islands of Tortola, Virgin Gorda, Anegada and Jost Van Dyke, along with more than 50 other smaller islands and cays. The capital, Road Town, is on Tortola, the largest island, which is about 20 km long and 5 km wide. British Virgin Islanders are British Overseas Territories citizens—and since 2002—are British citizens as well.

Getting to the Sunsail base on Tortola was less eventful than the trip to Göcek, Turkey, but still had its excitement. We flew from the USA into San Juan, Puerto Rico where we received a less-than-warm welcome into the region. After collecting our bags at the airport carousel, we were escorted into a little room and told to unpack our suitcases as uniformed men and women looked on and remonstrated with each other. We had absolutely no idea why they had targeted us or what was being said as the conversations were all in fast-paced Spanish. Thankfully nothing was found and we were sent on our merry way. Since then, I have been increasingly aware of the many young people being locked up in strange countries, having been accused of various crimes, most commonly the carrying of contraband. I am grateful that I was blissfully unaware of my own precarious situation at the time.

As with Turkey, the sailing in the BVI was also line-of-sight, requiring few charts and very little navigation ability as we could usually see the island we were heading towards. We did hit a few mild storms along the way, which meant the wind picked up for a while, but nothing serious. Mooring was easy, even if a little costly by our standards—in fact it was the only part of the world where we had been charged. We would pick up a buoy in one of the bays and pay USD20 to the owner. Typically, the owner was also the proprietor of the local restaurant which we often frequented.

Anegada, the northernmost island of the BVI, is the only inhabited BVI island formed from coral and limestone rather than of volcanic matter. While the other islands are mountainous, Anegada is flat and low. Its highest point is only about 28 feet (8.5 metres) above sea level, earning its name from the Spanish term for flooded land, *Tierra Anegada*. Due to the flat nature of the island, we could not rely on line-of-sight, and as we had no GPS to guide us, we used navigation points on the charts until we approached close enough to make out the sand mass.

Whilst Anegada is the second largest of the British Virgin Islands in area, it is also the most sparsely populated of the main islands, with most of the population living in the only village, named *The Settlement*. We moored at the village and made our way by taxi across the island to one of the beaches. We were the only people at the eating establishment on the beach and were treated like royalty while we relaxed over daiquiris and lobster. The return taxi ride was not quite as relaxing. Whilst one could call it memorable, it is not something I would want to repeat. The taxi was a utility vehicle and was shared with others—one person in the passenger seat up front and the rest of us in the open back. As we drove along, the laughter emanating from the cab led us to wonder what was going on. The person in the passenger seat decided to ply the driver with weed (yes—marijuana, cannabis or whatever you like to call it) as he drove. The next thing we knew, we had a flat tire. No matter how much we yelled out, the driver just kept driving … and very soon we were driving on the rim. This continued mile after mile until eventually we came across a little hamlet where we convinced the driver to stop so that we could hail another vehicle to get us back to the safety of our boat.

Let me guess—you would like to visit the Caribbean! Who wouldn't? Where would this location be on your list of priorities? How much do you believe it would contribute to what gives you joy?

Exploring the Amazon River and Rainforest

I had never contemplated floating on the Amazon River or traipsing through the Amazon Rainforest. It was only when planning an itinerary for a visit to Peru, that I realised that a section of the rainforest was in Peru and that it could be added on as a side trip.

Whilst some may think of the wild Amazon as adventurous and maybe even daunting, our trip to get there turned out to be almost as exciting as the time we spent there.

We were flying into Lima, Peru's capital city, via Madrid, Spain. After a delay in Spain, we arrived in Lima in the early hours of the morning. The considerable delay meant that there was no time for sightseeing and only a few hours to sleep before leaving for the airport. Anticipating touring the vibrant city, we had chosen to stay in a hotel in the beachside Miraflores area, which unfortunately, was further away from the airport. Before going to bed, we set an alarm, seriously concerned that we would not wake up in time to make our flight. An added complication was that we had no idea what time the flight was or how we were going to get to the airport. We expected that the travel agency would have left the information with the hotel. But alas, the staff at the front desk were equally in the dark. This was in the days before smartphones and we resorted to sending an email from the hotel computer, hoping that the somewhat dodgy internet connection would work sufficiently well to get the message to the travel agent.

I can still picture us sitting nervously in the breakfast room at the hotel, waiting for some kind of communication. Almost absentmindedly, Walter piped up, "I wonder if the black Mercedes there in the street is waiting for us." We peered out the window and on further investigation to our amazement, it was! We did not have much time to catch our flight but we packed up in record time, checked in at the airport, and boarded the flight to Puerto Maldonado—the gateway to the southern Amazon jungle.

The flight was followed by a rather arduous ride on the back of an old truck. We were required to get off at one point as the driver was concerned that the wooden bridge ahead would not hold the weight of both the truck and the passengers at the same time. On seeing the bridge, I had no idea how it would take the weight of the truck, let alone the weight of the rest of us. But somehow it did – first the truck, followed cautiously by the passengers.

The jarring truck ride was followed by a journey on a motorized canoe called a *bote*. Despite the pile of tasty rice that they served wrapped in a banana leaf, by the end of the two-hour voyage, I was hungry and uncomfortable after having spent more than enough time on the hard seat. I was eager to be off the boat and settled in our accommodation and even the steep path up through the mud from the river did not stop me from rushing to my final destination.

Our stay in Tambopata Reserve turned out well worth the drama and discomfort of getting there. It was even worth having to get up at 4 a.m. to go walking through the rainforest in gumboots supplied by the lodge—it was too sloshy for our hiking boots. We saw gigantic trees and tiny anthills; monkeys making their way through the treetops, and colourful macaws and other bright birds hurtling around the skies. Our guide even caught a piranha in the lake as we passed over in our raft-like vessel. The flesh-eating fish with enormous teeth was far smaller and less aggressive than I had imagined it would be. After showing it to us, the guide threw his prey back into the murky water. Although piranha attacks on people are considered rare, I was not in a hurry to have a swim in the lake, despite the extreme heat.

Another trip up the river on a *bote*–shorter this time and at night—provided all on board with Caiman sightings. Part of the alligator family, these creatures slide through the river, their eyes shining in the light of the guide's torch. Whilst typically preying on little animals and too small to attack humans, I was happy to watch them from afar under the watchful eye of our expert guide. We were also fortunate to catch a glimpse of the Capybara, a giant rodent native to South America. Whilst belonging to the same species as the domestic guinea pig, it is the largest rodent, growing to 106 to 134 cm (3.48 to 4.40 feet) in length, standing 50 to 62 cm (20 to 24 inches) tall, and typically weighing 35 to 66 kg. Although we only saw them along the shoreline at a distance, there was no concern about our safety as they are grass eaters.

The Amazon was an amazing experience, especially for a die-hard animal and bird lover. Would you be keen and willing to embark on a similarly unique adventure? What would make the discomfort worthwhile for you to go?

Riding a Camel

Have you ever ridden a camel? After having done so for the princely sum of five Australian Dollars on Dee Why Beach in Sydney, I still ask myself, "Why do so many people express a desire to want to ride a camel?" They are ungainly creatures that make for a less than-comfortable ride—and they smell! Perhaps if I was riding in a Bedouin train across the desert in North Africa or the Middle East, I may think of this activity as more thrilling than I do. And one day I may even do just that. But for now, yes, I've done it. I am happy I have done so—I think.

Would I jump at another opportunity—not likely. But if you have a desire to take a ride on this lumpy, bumpy animal, perhaps you should.

Have you done something purely because everyone else seems to wish to do so and it was readily available? Has it given you the satisfaction you expected based on the kudos given by others?

Cycling along the Danube

I was introduced to the "Blue Danube" as the famous waltz music by Johann Strauss when I was a dancer and aspiring musician. More recently, I had read about river cruises that sail up and down the river through cities such as Vienna and Budapest. I was not in a hurry to embark on such a cruise—partly because I was worried that if the river levels dropped, we would have to traverse the remainder of our journey on a bus. It was only when I took a short trip to Vienna whilst spending a few months in Italy, that I realised there was another alternative to seeing the area by river cruise ship.

After a few nights in the city of Vienna, Walter and I were looking forward to some time in the countryside, so we booked accommodation at a family inn in the Wachau Valley and hopped on the train for the trip to Krems an der Donau (Krems on the Danube). The Wachau (a UNESCO world heritage site located on the Danube River midway between the towns of Melk and Krems) attracts connoisseurs and epicureans for its high-quality wines. The valley is 36 kilometres in length and was settled in prehistoric times. A well-known town and popular tourist attraction is Dürnstein, where King Richard the Lionheart of England was held captive by Duke Leopold V of Austria and Styria. The architectural elegance of Dürnstein's ancient monasteries (Melk Abbey and Göttweig Abbey), castles and ruins—combined with the urban architecture of its towns and villages, and the cultivation of vines—are the dominant features of the valley.

Katharina picked us up at Krems station and took us to the lodgings run by her family, situated on the side of the Danube amongst apricot trees and vines. As we sipped on a cold glass of apricot bubbly, we received a warm welcome from Katharina's parents, Ilse and Adie, before being shown to our room. The room was decorated in apricot colouring—we were soon to find out that the *marille* (apricot) is central to the region and to the Aufreiter family business. Everything was apricot. *Marille* jam, wine, soap, liqueur, chocolate.

Following a hearty breakfast the next morning, Adie set us up with bicycle rentals and we set off on the 40+ kilometre ride to the town of Melk. Passing through little villages and alongside vines laden with grapes—it was the middle of harvesting—we followed the river, stopping along the way to enjoy the view. Melk is renowned for its Benedictine Abbey and we parked the bikes, climbed the steep hill up to the colourful structure and had a look around the outside. Time was not on our side—we had 50 kilometres to cycle home—so we chose not to pay the entrance fee to visit the inside of the abbey. We crossed the Danube and cycled back to the inn on the opposite bank.

Having joked that we had only seen a river that looked green, we took the recommendations of friends and family: drink more wine, wear polarised sunglasses, and continue your quest for the blue one. Whilst the colour of the river did not change, we did manage to find a blue building—the Stift Dürnstein (the abbey church at Dürnstein) was sky blue with a tall tower extending high in the air. It definitely stood out when we took a steep hike up the hill to the Burgruine Dürnstein, the ruined castle above the town. The view of the river and valley was worth every step.

Whilst there had been a fair bit of rain overnight, by the time we finished breakfast the next morning, it had stopped and we cycled up the steep hills through the vineyards behind the inn to the Göttweig Abbey. We decided not to join the guided tour as it was in the German language, but we spent an hour or so wandering around the part of the complex that is open to tourists. (The rest of the facility is inhabited by a group of Benedictine monks and off limits to tourists.)

When we arrived back, we found out that the family had a tasting at their winery that evening before dinner. After a rest and shower, we took a slow stroll along the road through the village. As we did so, a procession of cars from a wedding party passed by, honking their horns. For a brief moment, it made us feel as though we were getting a taste of real village life rather than experiencing what can seem to be artificially-created tourist activities.

We had a limited idea of what was going on at the tasting as the conversation was entirely in German. That said, our knowledge of Afrikaans did help us catch a few things as the language we grew up with in South Africa has some similarities to German. Regardless, the language challenge did not stop us from enjoying the wines, chocolates, and liqueurs on offer. When we returned to the inn for dinner, our hosts continued to fill our glasses with apricot wine and liqueur. A fun night was had by all and we retreated to bed feeling a bit the worse for wear.

On our final morning, we chose to head to the station early as we knew there was a marathon finishing in Krems and the roads would be blocked. The road closures turned out in our favour as—after having to walk a little way from where the taxi was forced to drop us off— we meandered down to the finish line and watched the competitors coming in. We were too early for the full marathon, but did see the quarter marathon (11 kilometres) competitors and as we headed back to the station with our bags, we were passed by the leaders of the half marathon.

We certainly were able to take in many experiences within a short time. This would not have been possible had we not been cycling. One of the benefits of being fit is that it allows you to take advantage of such activities when they present themselves.

How has your overall health affected your choice of adventures or activities? Is there something within your control that you can do that will allow you to do more or take hold of opportunities when they arise?

Cycling the Vancouver Seawall

Running is my go-to activity whenever I visit somewhere. It is convenient to put on a pair of runners and get out to explore. With cycling, however, more ground can be covered than on foot. Depending on the country, the stumbling blocks tend to be either financially related or the regulations and inconveniences regarding helmets. Hiring a bicycle in many places is much more expensive than renting a car. In the places where helmets are compulsory, I am not overly excited about wearing one that someone else has perspired in.

During our extended stay in Canada, Walter and I chose to invest in bicycle helmets. While visiting family on Vancouver Island and then with friends in Ottawa, they loaned us their bikes, enabling us to get out and about easily to explore all the nooks and crannies that many people never get to see. We did hire bicycles and helmets to explore Vancouver before purchasing said headwear. I was comfortable with renting helmets this one time as the bicycle shop had only just started the hire operation and we were able to pick out brand new helmets to rent. Renting the bicycles was also much cheaper than through other hire operations as the new business owners were trying to make their way into the market. After being kitted out with bike locks and our new helmets, we set off across the Burrard Bridge, a four-lane, Art Deco style, steel-truss bridge constructed in 1930–1932.

Hoping to cycle the length of the seawall, our first priority was Stanley Park, and we set off in that direction. Stanley Park is considered to be one of the great urban parks of the world, with 400 hectares of rainforest, manicured lawns, gardens, sports fields, beaches and trails. The seawall in Vancouver is a stone wall that was constructed around the perimeter of Stanley Park to prevent the erosion of the park's foreshore. Colloquially, the term also denotes the 30 kilometres pedestrian, bicycle, and rollerblading pathway that runs on the seawall and then further far beyond the boundaries of Stanley Park.

During the morning of our ride on the seawall, the wind built up, making it tough going at times, and a bit cool. But that did not detract from the experience. Leaving Stanley Park, we followed the seawall under the three bridges towards the Rogers Arena, the home of the Vancouver Canucks hockey team. The path circled past Science World towards the Olympic Village. The Vancouver Olympic Village, built for the 2010 Winter Olympics and 2010 Winter Paralympics, had over a thousand units able to accommodate over 2,800 athletes, coaches, and officials. There was a huge dragon boating event taking place, so we stopped to absorb the atmosphere. The fast and furious sport of dragon boat racing is a spectacle to watch with the colourful boats full of people paddling through the water at high speed.

Once again, cycling provided us with the opportunity to get closer to the action than we could by car whilst also covering a good distance. Cycling is a great way to explore a new place. If by some chance you do not know how to ride a bike, no need to despair. A good friend of mine learned to cycle at the age of 40 and my cousin in Canada did multi-day, long-distance (500 kilometres) cycling road trips into his 80s. So, it is never too late to learn and never too late to ride.

Is there a skill that you have always wanted to learn? Have you determined that it is too late to do so? Is now the time to rethink that decision and give it a go?

Flying With the Angels

I would love to take a poll—asking whether anyone reading this book has ever heard of the Volo dell 'Angelo. I certainly had never heard of it before planning a driving trip around this lesser-visited part of Italy and no one I have spoken to since my adventure has heard of the location either. I came across it almost inadvertently as I was searching for things to do whilst we were visiting Matera.

Above the Lucanian Dolomites, a mountain range in the heart of Basilicata, an hour's drive from the cave town of Matera, is a steel cable suspended between the tops of two small towns, Castelmezzano and Pietrapertosa, lets you live a unique experience called "Il Volo dell 'Angelo" (Flight of the Angel) We decided to spend the second day of our stay in Matera "flying."

With the road we had taken to Matera having been largely flat and dry, we were staggered by the rapid change in topography and vegetation on our way to Pietrapertosa, the village where we would begin our zipline flight. It was a main road, so we could relax and enjoy—that is, until the last 10 kilometres, where the wide flat roadway turned into a steep ascent up the mountain.

As we approached the start village for the first flight, the view of the return flight (the second one we would do) caused our heart rates to go up and some hyperventilation. We could see the coloured balls on the wire of the zipline stretching far across the enormous valley.

Tied side by side with a harness and attached to a steel cable, we had the thrill of flying across the beautiful landscape at a significant height—and at an astonishing speed! Twice! The first flight, known as the "San Martino" line, starts from Pietrapertosa at an altitude of 1,020 metres and travels across the valley to Castelmezzano at an altitude of 859 metres after covering a distance of 1,415 metres with a top speed of 110 km/hour. That is a lot of numbers, so to make it simple—it was very fast, very far, and very high off the ground! The velocity is equal to the maximum speed limit for vehicles travelling on many of the world's motorways. At the end of this first flight, the "angels" were brought back down to earth in Castelmezzano and freed from the harness. We reached the station of the return line by shuttle and a steep walk. The "dream" began again as we were suspended between heaven and earth during the return flight. The "Peschiera" line starts from Castelmezzano at an altitude of 1,019 meters and arrives in Pietrapertosa at an arrival altitude of 888 metres, covering 1,452 meters with a top speed even greater than the first flight—120 km/hour.

What an exhilarating experience—and not for the faint-hearted. Given the jolt when being brought to a stop at the end of each flight, I would suggest it is not for anyone with back issues either!

Are you feeling as though you are in a rut? As you get older, have you become increasingly risk-averse and scared to take a chance? Is there something that you can do to challenge and stretch yourself a little?

Summary

On reflection, it has been interesting to identify the things that I have chosen to do despite the risk. At times it has surprised me to discover the things that others would never do because they considered them too risky. Only in retrospect have I recognised that I have a fairly high level of risk tolerance—sometimes to the point of what others may think of as lunacy.

I have also enjoyed learning new skills for the express purpose of being able to take advantage of a particular opportunity. For example, whilst sailing has not become my sport of choice, it has enabled me to spend time on the water in various parts of the world. Not only have I found this more unusual mode of travel relaxing, it has stirred my desire to experience different cultures.

POINTS FOR REFLECTION

Identify those things that you **have done** in your life that you realise required taking a slightly higher level of risk than others would be willing to take. Give yourself kudos!

Identify those things that you **have done** in your life that you would not have been able to do without some effort to gain additional skills. Celebrate them!

Is there something you would still like to do that requires a new skill? How important is it to you?

9

Groundwork and Grit

We have already established that some things that we dream of doing can be done relatively easily, whenever we choose to do them or when the opportunity arises. Yet others require some level of risk taking, skill development or preparation.

Finally, there are activities and endeavours that rely on high levels of risk taking and skill development in addition to persistence and dogged determination to see them through. A large number of my experiences described in this book are physical challenges, requiring mainly physical preparation. There may be other forms of preparation, such as mental, emotional, and even financial.

In previous chapters dealing with the "Top 20," I described my marathon running achievements and the adventure of climbing Kilimanjaro. These activities required extensive physical and mental preparation. They also called on my tenacity, discipline, and downright pig-headedness to see them through to the end.

In this chapter, I will share several other pursuits that required risk taking, some that involved high levels of skill acquisition and preparedness, as well as others that entailed dedication and persistence.

Performing at the Sydney Opera House

Prior to my brother moving there, if I thought about an image of Sydney, Australia, either the Sydney Harbour Bridge or the Opera House would come to mind. However, my first in-person viewing of the Opera House can be best described as underwhelming. Not only was it substantially smaller than I had expected, but I had no idea that the Opera House was a series of "sails" rather than one large building. That said, there is something striking about the famous icon, and it still gives me a thrill to sail or take a ferry past this magnificent building jutting into Sydney Harbour or to run around the path surrounding the structure.

Designed by Danish architect Jørn Utzon, the building was formally opened on 20 October 1973 after a long gestation beginning with Utzon's 1957 selection as winner of an international design competition. The government's decision to build Utzon's design is often overshadowed by the circumstances that followed, including cost and scheduling overruns as well as the architect's ultimate resignation.

The building and its surrounds occupy the whole of Bennelong Point on Sydney Harbour, between Sydney Cove and Farm Cove. Bennelong Point sits adjacent to the Sydney central business district and the Royal Botanic Gardens, and near the world-famous, coat-hanger-shaped Sydney Harbour Bridge. It is perhaps due to the proximity to the now gigantic buildings of the CBD that the world-renowned structure is dwarfed.

Much as I love theatrical productions, it was almost five years after my move to Sydney before I attended a performance at this iconic landmark. My first entrance into the Concert Hall was from the rabbit warren of the backstage directly onto the stage as a performer in a small dance group. We were invited on two occasions to be part of a music and dance extravaganza celebrating positive relationships between Jewish and Christian communities. Somehow, the rather run-down dressing rooms were not what I had expected from this iconic building.

I am unlikely to perform there again. But I have done more than I could have ever dreamed of and far more than would ever have made its way to any *bucket list.*

Do you seek out opportunities to do things that you have never even thought possible? What have you done that has come about because you have looked for the chance and had the ability to take advantage of it when it revealed itself?

Traversing the Andes to Machu Picchu

Machu Picchu is a 15th-century Inca citadel located near the town of Cuzco in southern Peru. The Urubamba River flows past it, creating a canyon with a tropical mountain climate. Most archaeologists believe that Machu Picchu was constructed as an estate for the Inca emperor Pachacuti (1438–1472) and is the most familiar icon of the Inca civilization. The Incas built the estate around 1450 but abandoned it a century later at the time of the Spanish conquest. Although known by the locals, it was not known to the Spanish during the colonial period and remained generally unknown to the outside world until American historian Hiram Bingham brought it to international attention in 1911.

Over the years, I have seen photos of this icon of polished dry, stone walls and imagined what it must be like to be there in person, to feel the wonder and magnitude of the place. There was something about it that beckoned me. If I had possessed a machine to "beam me there," I would have done so. However, with South America being pretty far off the beaten track and not high on my list of priorities, I did not consider the possibility of going there.

As I was planning one of our end-of-year trips from Australia to see family in South Africa, I investigated where in the world we could go after Christmas. I was not particularly keen to experience the cold of the Northern Hemisphere, so Europe and North America were out of the question. The Southern Hemisphere became the prime contender and very soon, South America was chosen. To this day, I have no recollection as to why I honed in on Peru. Internet searches were unheard of at the time, so I relied on word-of-mouth and travel agent brochures for information.

Almost inadvertently, I connected with an Australian who ran a small travel agency in Peru with her Peruvian boyfriend. Whilst most visitors tend to embark on the popular and very touristed Inca Trail, Jane's company, Ultimate Tours, offered a trek to Choquequirao, a lesser-known Incan site in southern Peru similar in structure and architecture to Machu Picchu. We were to have the benefit of seeing both sites as after visiting the lesser-known Choquequirao, we would make our way across the Andes to the renowned Machu Picchu.

After making our way to Cusco, we spent a couple of days acclimatising to the altitude before embarking on the eight-day hike to Choquequirao and Machu Pichu. The evening before our departure on the trek, someone from the tour company visited us at the hotel to check our gear. At the time, our understanding was that he would be our guide. The following morning at 4:30 a.m., two men whom we had never met arrived at the hotel door and ushered my husband and I into a small vehicle already laden with people. The man from the evening before was nowhere in sight. It was a little disconcerting being taken away in the dark by a group of people we had not set eyes on before. After a short drive, another stranger—soon to be introduced as Mauro our guide—joined us. We soon realised that this was our team for the trek, including the cook that was sitting in the boot of the small vehicle with a large gas bottle.

Cachora, the starting point of the trek, was a couple of hours' drive from Cuzco. Unfortunately, getting a flat tyre whilst halfway along the route delayed us. We did not have a spare—there was no space to carry one of those—but our team managed to negotiate with a taxi driver to take us the rest of the way. We sat in the back of the taxi, closing our eyes as he navigated the misty, winding roads to where we would start our walk.

The only way to get to Choquequirao was via a tough climb up steep switchbacks and across swollen rivers. Due to the technical challenges of the terrain, porters were unable to carry the heavy gear, so horses were loaded up with all that was required for the journey. Our guide, Mauro, rallied the troops, made sure the horses were loaded with all the equipment, and issued the necessary instructions to the team. Soon Walter and I were following him into the beautiful green slopes of the Andes Mountains. The rest of the team would follow with the horses, food, tents, gear and—of course—the gas bottle that the cook had been nursing.

The first couple of days of our walk through the Andes to reach Choquequirao were spectacular—sunshine, blue skies, and condors soaring overhead. We arrived at Choquequirao mid-afternoon and explored the ruins set on the terraces that cascade down the mountain.

As Choquequirao was discovered far more recently than Machu Picchu, there was work still being done to unearth what lay below. Even so, there were no other people there–not one. It was just Mauro, Walter, and myself—and a few condors!

The site itself is frequented by very few people—at the time only approximately 150 people per year made the journey. For years, there has been talk by the Peruvian government of building a cable car to take tourists to this treasure, but this has yet to eventuate. In my opinion, I hope it never does. The solitude that we experienced when we arrived at the site would be spoilt by an influx of visitors. Other adventurers would not be able to experience the elation we felt by being the only visitors. The serenity was just reward for the hard work involved in getting there.

During the second night of our trek, following our afternoon visit to the ruins of Choquequirao, the heavens opened. Thunder howled and lightning thrashed as the rain bucketed down on our little tent. At times, I was convinced we were going to slide down the edge of the cliff on which we were precariously perched. Fortunately, we survived the night and the following morning had another opportunity to visit Choquequirao. This time, our only company were wild horses running around in the mist.

The remainder of our trek to Machu Picchu was wet, muddy and slippery. Numerous landslides meant that we had to navigate the edges of cliffs, a few times depending on Mauro's strong and steady hand to guide us across. Even more frightening were the river crossings! Typically, I love the sound of running water, but I could feel myself stiffen up every time I heard the noise of rushing cascades. Rock hopping across the rivers was treacherous and where bridges had existed, most had been washed away. The sound of the river rushing through Agues Calientes, the end of the trek and the kick-off point for the bus to Machu Picchu, kept me awake rather than relaxing me. The decision to choose the destination based on weather may have helped us avoid the cold Northern Hemisphere, but we definitely had not taken into consideration the wet season in Peru—complete with its torrential rain and landslides.

In an odd way, one of the highlights of the time high in the mountains between Choquequirao and Machu Pichu came about because of the rain. Our food tent was soaked, so one of the local Quechua families graciously offered for us to share their home with them for our evening meal. As we sat at the table eating our casserole, the family's guinea pigs ran around our feet, meat carcasses hung from the ceiling and the members of the family—ranging from a six-week-old baby to the more than one-hundred-year-old grandfather—munched on their potatoes by the fire (there are over 300 varieties of potato in Peru). After the meal, I spent time with the teenage daughter in the household, helping her with English homework—together we did a reasonable job of translating Spanish into English.

The final part of our journey was by bus. After a much-needed shower and a night in a real bed in a hotel, we caught the first bus out of Aguas Calientes, arriving at Machu Picchu in the early morning mist, before most of the tourists. This was the place I had seen in pictures. Now I was a part of those pictures, standing there, breathing in the damp air and smelling the surrounding vegetation. We spent hours wandering around the site with the wild llamas that call the ruins their home. A surreal experience that I will be hard-pressed to forget.

I have never regretted my visit to Machu Picchu—it surpassed all expectations. Would I do it again? In a heartbeat! Would I take on the trek to Choquequirao to get there? I am less sure about that. Despite my level of fitness and ability to push through, it was one of the more arduous things I have done, particularly given the wet conditions. I chose this trek because I knew it was considerably tougher than the Inca Trail and would test me. I am also someone who rebels against following the crowd and will choose something different almost on principle. The downside is that I have been able to receive very little kudos for this endeavour, so if I did it only to gain applause from others, I failed. Many people know of the Inca Trail, but few have heard of Choquequirao, and even fewer know the hostile walking conditions and limited facilities in the remote mountain area.

My dream turned into a reality. It also ignited new passions for trekking that led to new adventures.

Is there something you have always dreamed of doing? What is your reason for doing it? Is it your passion? Is it for the kudos of others? Have you done something that was tougher than expected? Was it worth it?

Trekking to Everest Base Camp

I spent hours checking out options for climbing Kilimanjaro, including researching the different routes, trekking companies, and weather patterns. Having chosen an operator, selected the route and selected September / October as the best time of the year, it was time to book. But then our situation changed. The Kilimanjaro climb was put on the back burner.

When the 2012 financial crisis hit, Walter and I both had work contracts suspended during the first half of the year. We had two choices. Option one was to worry about spending money, stop travelling and search desperately for other clients and sources of income. Option two was to take advantage of the downtime and go off on an adventure. A friend was joining a group heading off to trek to Everest Base Camp (EBC). Within days, we established that there were two spots available, signed up and paid for the trek, booked flights to Kathmandu, and reserved a hotel room in Nepal's capital city. I had done no research, had no idea of the itinerary, and did not even know whether the operator was sound. I must tell you that this is very unusual for me. Whilst I do embark on many activities and adventures, I am seldom rash. I spend considerable time programming data into my brain to turn it into decision-making information when required. This time I had nothing, zip, zilch!

Fortunately, in spite of my lack of research, my experience turned out to be far superior to what the majority of trekkers experience! I had no idea that most trekking groups do not have the opportunity to stay over at Base Camp. They arrive at the rock that states "Everest Base Camp," take photos and embark on the downward journey. Having seen photos of EBC, I had not realised that a significant number of people that make the expedition to EBC do not even see the little yellow tents dotted around the rocky, icy terrain.

Unless you make the journey during the limited Everest climbing season (usually April/May and possibly October), there are no tents—as there are no climbers. Those that use EBC as a base to acclimatise and prepare for climbing to the summit of the world's highest mountain pay copious amounts of money to cover the expense required to set up and maintain the extensive facilities that include the tents. These committed mountaineers also spend months at EBC. It is too expensive and requires too many resources to haul everything up and down the rough tracks for the short visits paid by the trekkers. Laden helicopters cannot make it up to that altitude safely. Sherpas have to carry everything up and down. (And I mean everything! That includes all the garbage as well as the waste emitted by each person when they visit the toilet tent, what we endearingly called the "rocket". Our grateful thanks to the porters who drew the short straw!)

As our operator had climbers attempting to summit Everest that year, they had already set up the infrastructure to house said hardcore adventurers whilst they did their acclimatisation. So, we had the amazing privilege of spending two nights in one of those little yellow numbers. The temperature dropped drastically overnight. No way were we going to the rocket in minus 5 degrees Celsius (thank goodness for pee bottles). During the night it was eerie hearing the avalanches and hoping none would come down on us.

But the upsides far outweighed any discomfort. We were treated to fresh apple pie and other amazing cooking in the warm meal tent and we had fun checking out the crevasses and sliding down the ice leading to the notorious Khumbu Icefall. The Khumbu Icefall is located at the head of the Khumbu Glacier and the foot of the Western Cwm, a broad, flat, gently undulating glacial valley basin on the Nepali slopes of Mount Everest, not far above Base Camp and southwest of the summit. The icefall is considered one of the most dangerous stages of the Nepalese route to Everest's summit.

We discovered that getting to Lukla, the start of the EBC trek is not for the faint-hearted. There are two choices: one involving several days of trekking and the other being a 30-minute flight from Kathmandu. A short flight seems to be a no-brainer—and that is what our group chose.

Forbes magazine describes Lukla airport as the most dangerous in the world. Airports can be challenging for pilots for many reasons. Sometimes it is the short runway, whilst in other instances it is strong winds or it could be the sheer, mountainous terrain. Yet another issue is the high altitude, which presents a danger due to the effect that low air density has on the handling of an aeroplane. Guess what! Lukla has all of these four issues! No wonder one of our fellow climbers— not a big fan of flying at the best of times—was in tears during the short flight. Being an avid adventure seeker and aspiring pilot, I loved sitting near the front of the plane watching the instruments light up with "Danger, danger" as we approached the mountain at the end of the short runway before taking a dramatic swerve to the right.

The flight from Lukla back to Kathmandu is known to be a bit of a bun fight with lots of people milling around everywhere, gesticulating, shouting and pushing to ensure that they get on their flight. Frequent fog and other weather issues have been known to delay trekkers for days, but with a clear morning, we were soon on our way. The only excitement was the drop-off at the end of the downhill runway before soaring up over the mountains—another idiosyncrasy of this crazy airport.

We did have a little more excitement at the end of the trip. Nepal was in a time of political upheaval and violent protests had sprung up around Kathmandu, blocking many of the roads. We were fortunate that the hotel was able to arrange a military escort for us from our accommodation in the nation's capital to the airport. We left the kingdom of Nepal making our way home after an exhilarating experience.

I still nurture fond memories of sitting in a German bakery in the village of Tengboche—one of our overnight stops on the way to EBC— having an apple cake with Walter for his birthday and continuing the celebration with the team later that night. One of the porters had lugged a cake, in its box, all day from the bakery in the previous overnight stop of Namche Bazaar.

I still recall—although not as fondly—the cough that Walter and I caught on the trip and held on to for six weeks following the adventure. I also developed a chest infection and made a visit to the hospital at EBC. Perhaps the illness was exacerbated when I was caught in a severe thunderstorm during the final day of walking, arriving at our accommodation at the typical Nepalese tea house in Lukla in drenched clothes. As the porters carrying our bags had not arrived yet, the only things I had to put on my icy feet were the down mittens I had been carrying in my backpack. It is a good thing that these memories have become stories and the pain and inconvenience experienced at the time have disappeared.

For many people, being this close to Everest would tempt them to attempt to summit. Even then, I had no desire to climb it. I was glad I made it to base camp at its altitude of 5,364 metres. It is close enough and I feel no need to risk life and limb for the additional 3,000 metres. But kudos to those that do!

Have you done something challenging and realised that you have reached the risk level to which you are prepared to go? How does that make you feel? Are you able to give others credit for taking greater risks in achieving their dreams?

Tackling Hikes, Tramps, and Mountain Summits

In Italy - Climbing Mount Mongioie (2,630 metres)

Liguria is a crescent-shaped region in northwest Italy. Its Mediterranean coastline is well known for the five colourful fishing villages of the Cinque Terre: Monterosso al Mare, Vernazza, Corniglia, Manarola, and Riomaggiore. This UNESCO heritage site draws hundreds of tourists from across the globe to marvel at its beauty. I was fortunate to have the opportunity to traverse the rugged steep landscape along the mountain tracks that join the villages during a short trip to Italy to celebrate our 20th wedding anniversary. Liguria is not only bordered by coastline but is home to beautiful mountain ranges, with the Ligurian Alps forming the border with the region of Piedmont.

A few years after our hike between the villages of the Cinque Terre, we watched an episode of the television show "Escape to the Continent" that featured Liguria and mentioned a walking company. We made contact with the owner, an Italian who had spent considerable time in the UK and spoke English well. We kept in touch and were happy to have his knowledge when we ventured to Liguria again. Whilst we were happy to embark on a couple of short trails on our own, not knowing the terrain or conditions, we were more reticent about embarking on a more strenuous walk, especially the climb to the summit of Mount Mongioie that we had spotted near the village of Viozene, not far from where we were staying. All it took was a quick email (okay, maybe a few emails) to our Italian friend to lock in the details and we were on our way to the town of Pieve di Teco to pick up Lorenzo.

We had no phone or internet reception, so finding Lorenzo was not straightforward. Fortunately, as we were walking around the streets of the small town trying to find him, Walter recognised him from the television episode we had watched several times. So, following a quick brioche and macchiato, we hopped in the car and drove to Viozene for the start of our climb.

As we approached the hamlet, we could see remnants of the snow that had fallen on the mountain overnight. We had unwittingly chosen the coldest day of our trip so far to climb to the summit at 2,600 metres! But the snow did make for a scenic walk, albeit slippery in a few spots.

We were privileged to spot (with Lorenzo's help) several marmots—little mountain creatures that live in burrows. Not so little at the time, but a bit rotund, as they were preparing for their winter hibernation. Luck was certainly on our side as we also saw several *camoscio* (chamois), a species of goat-antelope, skipping around the slopes. Lorenzo also had a chat to a cow that was sunning itself on the southern slope. It did not appear to appreciate being disturbed!

The view of the sea and the Ligurian Alps from the summit of the mountain made all the climbing, slipping and rock hopping worthwhile. We signed the summit book, placing our names alongside the other people that had achieved the same feat before us. We sat behind some rocks, sheltering from the cold wind, as we nibbled on our snacks. Unfortunately, we left our descent a few minutes too late—by the time we set out, the sun had all but disappeared behind the cloud. With the wind still blowing, we were glad for our gloves. But amazingly, the snow on the southern slopes had melted, giving us a very different view than it had been on our ascent.

We made a stop at a mountain refuge for a welcome (and well-earned) cappuccino. Filled with wooden beams and prayer flags, it felt a bit like entering a Nepalese tea house, bringing back memories of our trek through the Himalayas to Everest Base Camp. Even the person making the coffee was Nepalese!

The day ended with *aperitivi* with Lorenzo at a bar in Pieve. Being with a local, the accompanying free cheese, meat and bread snacks were likely much better than we would have had on our own! Since then, we have become good friends with Lorenzo and have appreciated his local expertise on several occasions.

In Argentina - Summiting Mount Lomas Blancas (3,650 metres)

Mendoza is a city in Argentina famous for its olive oil production and wine, notably Malbec. Located in a region of foothills and high plains on the eastern side of the Andes, it provides the opportunity to walk off some of the indulgences. After having spent a day cycling to a few wineries, drinking, and eating more than our fair share, we booked a tour to climb to the top of Mt Lomas Blancas. In this case, we did not have a Lorenzo to call on, so had to rely on a few internet searches to find a guide. On the day in question, we woke up to a rather misty and overcast day, causing some concern that our outing would be jeopardised. We went ahead with breakfast and gathered our hiking equipment together, ready for our 8:45 a.m. pickup. Our guide was perfectly on time and after loading our gear into his small car, he was whisking us out of town to the Cordon del Plata National Park. The starting point of our hike was some 100 kilometres away, taking about 1.5 hours, primarily due to the gravel switchback road for the last part of the trip.

Following the somewhat tedious final part of the drive, we were grateful to be able to stop and stretch our legs. We climbed out of the car, adjusted hiking poles and set out in the mist to climb to the top of Mt Lomas Blancas. As we moved on, the mist cleared and we were surrounded by blue skies and green fields splattered with grazing cows.

Then the blue disappeared, only to be replaced by another cloud of mist. This is how most of the ascent went—mist coming and going, with some extremely strong gusts of wind thrown in the mix. The wind was so strong that we could hear it coming.

It turned out to be a relatively easy climb, with very little rock hopping required. It still felt pretty good to make it to the top and enjoy the spectacular views over the nearby glacier to the carpets of mist filling the valleys.

After a banana and a couple of muesli bars, we were ready to start the descent. We took a more direct route down and the loose scree made it both challenging and fun—all three of us had a few slips. By the time we were down the main part of the mountain, the mist had come in thick, and we were glad to have a local experienced guide leading us the rest of the way. Soon we were back at the car and the trip back to the hotel sped by—we tried not to look at the speedometer!

As in Italy, a day out in Argentina would not be complete without more food and drink. And we deserved it after a mountain climb! As it was still relatively early—typically restaurants only open after 8 p.m.—we were a little limited in our choice, but we found a Parilla (Argentinian BBQ) to enjoy a steak and a bottle of Torrentes (white wine from the Salta province of Argentina). Our guide had recommended super dulce de leche gelato from a gelateria a few metres from our hotel, so that was dessert. Dulce de leche is a caramelised milk product originally from Latin America, and this gelato is not common in other parts of the world. Since being introduced to super dulce de leche gelato in Argentina, it has become our absolute favourite dessert and we have it whenever it is available. We have managed to track down a gelato shop in Rome that sells it and a chain of shops in Australia, so we are able to get our fix when we are in either of those locations.

In New Zealand – Tramping the Tongariro Crossing

Whilst our climbs up Mt Lomas Blancas and Mt Mongioie were tranquil and our only company was of the winged and four-legged variety, the same could not be said of the day we took on the Tongariro Alpine Crossing. This popular day hike is in Tongariro National Park on the North Island of New Zealand. The Tongariro National Park is a World Heritage site that has the distinction of dual status, as it has been acknowledged for both its natural and cultural significance. The Tongariro Alpine Crossing is heralded as the best one-day trek in New Zealand and is regarded as among the top ten single-day treks in the world. Many who complete the 19.4 kilometres journey will tell you the climbs can be steep and the weather unpredictable but worth it in every aspect.

The national park is rich in both cultural identity and dramatic, awe-inspiring natural scenery. Unique landforms, including the volcanic peaks of Ngauruhoe, Tongariro and Ruapehu ensure the Tongariro Alpine Crossing is considered a world-renowned trek.

Due to a shortage of parking because of the popularity of the route, and the fact that the hike does not end where it starts, we had no option but to book transport with a local operator. The almost full moon was still bright in the sky as we left our accommodation in the little town of Ohakune to meet the shuttle that would take us to the start of our hike. As we stood waiting, the dawn broke and we had our first view of the summit of Mt Ruapehu—it had been shrouded in mist since our arrival a couple of days prior. We could hear the birds waking as well as the cows, but still no sound of our transport. Just as we were about to check tickets for a contact number, we spotted the bright lights of the small bus coming down the road. "Whew, they have't forgotten us."

The bus was full of Brits, Swiss, Germans and Canadians. We were surprised that there were no other Australians on board. Within an hour, we were at the carpark, well briefed by the driver on what to expect, and on our way on the track. The first part of the tramp (typical New Zealand term for hike) was flat and easy, the only challenge being the narrow parts where passing was difficult. The track is so well built and maintained that it is a bit like a walker highway! We knew this was New Zealand's most popular day hike but wow, so many people!

Soon we reached the "Devil's Staircase"—so named for the very steep path climbing wooden stairs … up, up, up! As we ascended, we moved above the fog and the views opened up. Reaching the South Crater was our first achievement and after the descent on the other side, it was a treat walking across the huge, flat expanse before starting our next ascent.

The next climb was not quite as well paved, with a little rock hopping and scrambling required to reach the Red Crater. It was worth every step, rewarding us with views over the Emerald Lakes below, and revealing steam rising from the crater walls. After joining the throngs of people sliding down the scree slope on the other side of the climb (fortunately we refrained from joining some of them in falling), we took a break alongside one of the lakes. We nibbled on the pizza rolls we had brought for lunch, even though it was only 10:30 in the morning—but we did have breakfast at 6 a.m. so it was not too unreasonable.

The walk through the following craters filled with old lava flows was surreal. Soon after our final crater walk, we descended into the mist and for a few kilometres, we walked the monotonous switchback track.

The sighting of steam rising out of the Ketetahi hot springs was a welcome distraction from the tedium before we reached our next snack stop at the Ketetahi Shelter overlooking Lake Taupo, a large crater lake. The vista was lovely but the grandeur was reduced by the amount of mist shrouding the valley.

The final few kilometres were through a forest following a stream and we eventually came out of the bush—straight into a buzz of activity where those that had already completed the hike were waiting for their shuttles. As we had completed the walk in less than the average time, we had a long wait for the transport back to our accommodation. We had fun watching others finish amidst the hive of activity.

In Australia - Climbing Mount Kosciusko (2,228 metres)

Given Mount Kosciuszko is mainland Australia's tallest mountain and is one of the seven summits of the world (the Seven Summits are the highest mountains of each of the seven traditional continents), I would be remiss if I excluded this experience in this chapter. Not being skiers, it took us several years of living in Australia to get our act together to visit Thredbo at the base of Mount Kosciuszko and then wondered why we had never done so before. Even without snow in May, the popular Australian ski resort town was beautiful. In fact, we probably saw it as very few people have the opportunity to do— very quiet. May was definitely out of season—being after the summer mountain biking and hiking rush and before the winter ski season. The downside was that the restaurants and cafes were closed. The good thing was that we had most of the paved walking path to ourselves as we climbed to the summit of Australia's tallest mountain.

I am always ready to take on a trek or small mountain summit in different parts of the world. Do you have a niche activity or challenge that you love? Are you always ready to do it? If not, is there some base preparation that you can do?

Hiking the Larapinta Trail End-To-End

Whilst our climb up Mount Kosciuszko was fun, it was not particularly taxing. I cannot say the same about our trek along the Larapinta Trail in Australia's Northern Territory. Once again, this was something that Walter and I were only able to do because we had a certain amount of preparation under our belts. We were fit as a result of our running training and relatively well-equipped for hiking, having bought the gear for previous outings.

As described by our trekking company, Trek Larapinta, The Larapinta Trail is an extended bushwalking track running west from Alice Springs to Mount Sonder. Its 223 kilometres through the steep red slopes of the West MacDonnell Ranges National Park are fast gaining a reputation for offering one of the finest walking experiences in the world. The ranges rise dramatically from the Central Australian desert, typifying the rugged landscapes of the area—also known as the Red Centre—with the changing hues of the mountain peaks, rolling hills and dry river valleys made famous in the paintings of Albert Namatjira.

Whilst we had completed numerous day hikes and mountain summits in nearly every state in Australia, all our challenging multi-day adventures had been overseas. When Australia was in lockdown during the Covid epidemic and we were not allowed to leave the country, we had the perfect opportunity to do something locally. We soon discovered that many other Australians were thinking the same thing. On investigating our options for taking on the Larapinta Trail, we found we did not have any. The only two operators that offered the full end-to-end hike were full to the brim. With the 2020 season cancelled due to the pandemic, all the bookings had been moved out to 2021. In line with my typical approach, I was determined to do the full option, the hardest one—I could not possibly just go for the highlights package. That said, we certainly did not feel up to taking on the independent option. We had never hiked carrying a full pack before, and being such an arduous long trail, we would need to organise food drops along the way as we would never be able to carry sufficient provisions.

Being unable to book a place in a group to embark on the Larapinta Trail, we decided to register for the Brisbane Marathon at the beginning of June 2021. Having only done the half marathon in Brisbane in the past, we figured that as we were going to be there at the time, we might as well do the event—even if our last marathon had been in Paris five years earlier—and before my near-death experience with DVT and PE!

In February 2021, we were contacted by Trek Larapinta and offered two slots on a trip starting on 15 May. This meant that we would have less than two months to prepare for the hike and that we would finish the expedition exactly one week before the marathon. One could take this as 223 kilometres of training for the 42.2 kilometre run or view it as crazy to consider both. Known for our craziness, we decided to book our 16-day hike. Had we known the extent of the blisters we would develop from the arduous rocky track, we may have done otherwise—sometimes ignorance is bliss!

We completed a couple of training hikes to make sure our poles, backpacks and shoes were okay and to practise our technical skills. Other than that, we largely relied on our running and marathon training and general fitness. This went a long way to equip us with the physical and mental endurance to get us through the hike. It did nothing to prepare us for the hardcore life of sleeping in the open, going to the toilet in the bush, and spending 16 days without a shower, hair-wash, or shave.

Fortunately, we had most of the gear that we needed from previous excursions. We were in the process of moving and storing so we just had to make sure we did not pack it away when moving our other belongings into storage—and to find a way to manage so much extra stuff in our little Airbnb apartment. The process of sorting, moving and storing was a little like completing a jigsaw puzzle.

Getting to the Northern Territory was our first flight under Covid conditions and that meant wearing masks at the airport and on the planes. The day was long as we had to fly Brisbane-Melbourne-Alice Springs as there was only one direct flight a week and not on the day we needed—another consequence of Covid as many flights were cancelled. The plane from Melbourne to Alice was full—we found out later that there was a huge group of people doing a film / commercial.

We had a couple of nights at a hotel on the outskirts of Alice Springs prior to leaving for our hike. Having heard some horror stories about safety in Alice, we were happy that we did not experience anything untoward or sinister. That said, we avoided going out at night. During the day, we walked along the road parallel to the Todd River (a dry river bed) from our hotel into town where we enjoyed the quirky cafes. They served great coffee, good food and all the ones we visited had very interesting decor.

On day one of the booked trip, it was a bit of a shock when we were bundled with eight perfect strangers into the back of a Troopy—a Toyota Landcruiser workhorse—to rattle our way to the start of the trail at the Telegraph Station. It would likely have been confronting at any time, but after a year of social distancing, it was more than a little unnerving. It is funny how the vehicle seemed to grow over the 16 days together as we got to know each other intimately.

We were blessed to have a great bunch of people in the group from different ages (ranging from 28-71) and backgrounds. I can honestly say that not one person had led what could be termed a mundane life.

Speaking of intimacy, getting to know each other's toilet habits and changing clothes in front of the others (except the days when we stayed in one location for more than one night and had tents) became a norm. The tribal stench of bodies cleaned only with wet wipes or a bird bath (a few cm of boiling water in a bowl) must have been terrible for anyone else we came in contact with. Fortunately, that was not too often—only on some of the bigger trailheads where there were carparks. Whilst at camp, at least we did have a bucket in a little blue tent for doing number twos, so that afforded us some dignity. We also had a bowl of cold water for washing our hands. We did not wash them in the bowl but would use a cup to draw off a small amount to pour into a plastic container containing holes and hanging in a tree. We had to be very quick to put our hands covered in liquid soap under the container before all the water ran out. It was a total shock when we arrived at a carpark with a flushing toilet and running taps. And let's not mention looking in mirrors!

The first few nights were spent in swags set on top of tarps and open to the elements. Swags have long been used in Australia as a safe and comfortable way of sleeping underneath the stars whilst out trekking. Swags are essentially a man-size tent, being open sleeping bags made from canvas. They have a sponge-like mattress attached to the bottom to create a more comfortable experience. We then placed our sleeping bag within that to create heat and an extra layer of security. The good thing about them was that we were able to view the expansive sky full of twinkling stars. I saw more falling stars than I have seen in my life to date! The not-so-good thing was that icy wind built up and howled through the camp in the middle of the night and I thought it was going to cause frostbite on my cheeks as my face was exposed to the elements.

We were happy to erect tents when we were at a camp for more than one night. Only one swag would fit in a tent, so we set up two next to each other with the window open so we could see each other and chat. It gave the added benefit of being able to put all our bags and boots inside away from the dingoes that had been happy to play with the boots of other hikers on the trail.

Whilst rugged as one would expect from a desert, we were surprised by how much the scenery changed over the 16 days. As we traversed across valley floors and along mountain ridges, there was always something different to see. The much-needed rains earlier in the year had led to the blooming wildflowers, particularly vast plains of white and purple Mula Mula. As expected, the gaps, gorges and passes were spectacular. Sadly, the buffel grass imported from South Africa to reduce erosion had done what any introduced species tends to do; following extensive bushfires along the trail a couple of years before, the buffel grass had taken over vast areas that should have been full of spinifex. Although I thought it was unfortunate that the natural grasses had been decimated, I had to admit that coming up against a stalk of buffel grass is a lot softer on the bottom than spiny spinifex.

A friend who had completed some sections of the trail had told us he was surprised by how rocky it was. When he mentioned it, we thought he must be exaggerating and even if not, we would be able to easily navigate the terrain—after all, we had walked in so many locations and come across rocks before. But he wasn't kidding! The boulder hopping and navigation of rocks in the dry riverbeds was one thing. But the constant pounding of the rocks underfoot was relentless; even through thick boots, the balls of my feet started to throb. My boots took a beating and I had to make use of my spare pair after the first set came apart after just three days on the relentless stones. I am typically grateful that I never get blisters, even on a marathon. The Larapinta Trail's reputation for blisters is certainly not to be sneezed at. The incessant rolling of the feet across the rocky terrain caused movement in the boot and created blisters in places on my feet I did not think possible. As I read in an article on the trail: "There were blisters on blisters."

The first couple of days were sunny, but with icy winds continuing and building up during the nights. The temperatures then escalated, with one morning's minimum as high as 14 degrees Celsius. A brief stint of rain brought with it a returning bout of cold. Whilst the rain did not last, the cold did. Arriving at the summit of Mount Sonder for sunrise on the last morning of the trail, we were freezing cold and very grateful for the hot drinks that the guides had carried up for us.

The end of the trail was a bittersweet moment. Being able to have a shower and wash hair, sleep in a bed, and eat out of a china plate was bliss. Sorting out our dirty clothes was surprisingly cathartic.

Leaving my old hiking boots in the garbage bin in the hotel room was sad. They had travelled with me to Everest Base Camp, Kilimanjaro, Antarctica, Argentina and New Zealand. Sadly, the first three days of the Larapinta Trail had proven too much for them.

After being in such close quarters, it was strange to be separating, never to be together as a group again. Many of us met at the airport the following day, as we were all on the same flight out to Sydney, and bid final farewells.

A few days after getting back, we managed a run—the muscle memory worked. And a week after completing the trail, we ran the Brisbane Marathon together, finishing in a respectful—if not speedy—time of 4 hours and 22 minutes.

I would do the Larapinta Trail again in a heartbeat! Even with the hygiene challenges and cold mornings! Since the trip, I have whetted the appetite of several people who would like to attempt the hike—if not in whole, certainly in part.

I had the physical fitness to take on the trip but had underestimated the living conditions. Have you done something that you thought you were prepared for and were not? How did it turn out?

Completing the Vancouver and Banff Half Marathon

Shortly after arriving in Canada for our three-month trip, we completed the Vancouver Half Marathon. It was a great day out. A fabulous way to be part of the local running community, enjoy the scenery of Stanley Park, run past the site of the 2010 Winter Olympics, and even run across the Cambie Bridge. I was recovering from a minor operation at the time and had been training deprived, so was happy to enjoy the day out and finish with a respectful time. It was definitely a day to remember and something I am grateful to have had the opportunity to take part in.

Whilst we were on this three-month journey, we saw that there was a half Marathon in Banff around the time we would be visiting. Oh well—why not?! We changed our plans and extended our stay to complete this run—and we were glad we did. The atmosphere was fun, the temperature was ideal and the views were spectacular.

On the day of the event, there was great weather—a sunny day and reasonably warm temperature. The run only started at 9:30 a.m.—rather late for a run in our books. With having done little running due to all our travelling and my recent illness, we decided to take it easy and enjoy the day out. Well, that was the plan. Somehow my body had another idea—and I took off at a quicker pace than I intended. Some days you just need to run at what feels right, but I was concerned that I would pay for this in the second half.

The course was great with beautiful scenery and there was a reasonable field size in the event. Not so great was that most of the course was spectator-free. With access closed to cars, bikes and other pedestrians, there was little support and cheering along the way for encouragement. In the lead up, there was talk about bears and whether to carry "bear spray" (mace). We decided we would not bother—we figured that if a bear gets close enough to require us to use bear spray, we have bigger issues. I am glad to report we did not encounter any bears on the run.

The backdrop was stunning and I focused on the beauty rather than any pain. The middle third of any run is often the hardest, but we were able to keep a good pace. Unlike the start and middle of the race, towards the end, we had spectator support and the cheering helped keep us going. And so, despite little training, we were able to complete this run somewhat quicker than the one we ran in Vancouver.

I get goosebumps every time I see the photo of me running along the glacial lake outside Banff township under turquoise blue skies and with a snow-covered peak behind

I enjoy running events so ensure I keep as fit as possible. What do you enjoy doing? Think back on the times you have been able to do something when the opportunity has arisen, purely because you have been ready. How have you felt when you have had to miss out?

Paying Off a Mortgage

I realise that most of my stories are about globetrotting activities and adventures. There are other stories of achievement that I could have included but have not. But as it is the outcome of the following story that has enabled me to do most of the things that I have written about, I decided it was worth including.

In my early 30s, at what I am going to call the pinnacle of my business career, I had one of Australia's well-known financial services companies as a client. In particular, the person who had engaged me was on top of his game, an expert in investment markets and products. Amongst our many academic and life conversations, I clearly remember him saying that he wanted to pay his mortgage off by the age of 40. Somehow that resonated with me, so Walter and I met with his financial adviser at the time and put the wheels in motion. Whilst we did not meet the age deadline for paying off the debt, what it did do was provide a goal and instil discipline. It meant that we made a choice not to buy the biggest, most expensive house or upgrade—we funnelled every spare cent into the mortgage. By the time we had paid off our mortgage – not long after the targeted age - we also had years of budgeting and expense information with which to make informed decisions on future spending. Whilst acknowledging that I have been blessed with so much, the financial saving, recording and discipline have been instrumental in giving Walter and me the flexibility to do the things we want to do.

Is there a single but significant factor that could prevent you from reaching for your dreams? If so, is there someone you can reach out to help you tackle it?

Moving to Italy

Having moved countries when relocating from South Africa to Australia and spent up to three months at a time living in various places in the world—Canada, Argentina and Italy—I still had a desire to make another move. Ever since selling my home in Sydney, Australia, following my DVT/PE, I have been transient. But I had a dream. A long-term move to Italy. It was only as I started working through the planning did I realise the obstacles to such a relocation. At the time, the difficulties were magnified with Covid. As an Australian, I was not allowed to leave the country during the height of the pandemic. I am not sure if this prevention gave me an extra incentive to move— like a caged animal pushing against the bars—or my rebellious nature wanting to do it because I was told I was not allowed to do so. But by the time borders opened, flights were booked, leases were signed, and visas were in place. Having spent a year in Florence, the home of Renaissance art and architecture, my husband and I now live in the centre of the small walled city of Lucca, also in Tuscany.

Have you had something that you have dreamt about doing, perhaps for years, but there have always been too many obstacles in place? Are those same restrictions still there or have circumstances changed sufficiently to make it possible? What do you need to do in order to turn it into a reality?

Summary

From when I was a child, sport, dancing and a need to always be moving kept me fit. Fitness is a passion, an obsession, a part of my DNA. As I have maintained a high level of fitness throughout the years, there have been times when I have been able to embark on an adventure or do an activity when the opportunity presented itself. This has afforded me the ability to do things with very little lead time. That does not mean there has not been the need for targeted or accelerated training in the lead-up to an event, but having a solid base has certainly been invaluable and widened our choices.

In addition to physical fitness, going through challenging endeavours has also tested and developed my level of determination and discipline. They have cultivated the mental strength to match the physical.

I strongly recommend that you be prepared for the things that most interest you. Save the money, build the skills, foster the mental capacity. Do not wait until the opportunity arises—you may find yourself not sufficiently fit or without an essential skill to take advantage of the opportunity.

There are many areas in life that we are required to take risks in order to learn, advance or success. My high-risk tolerance and relative lack of fear have enabled me to embark on activities that others may deem to be life-threatening. That said, I have a fear of failure which has been a consistent challenge for me to overcome. The real secret to success is not about trying to avoid adversity and obstacles. It lies in our ability to embrace challenges and use them to learn from and propel us towards our desired results.

POINTS FOR REFLECTION

Think about those things you have completed or achieved through pure grit, determination and discipline or things that have required preparation or practice. These may be physical pursuits, but do not have to be.

Think about those things that you have missed out on because you were not prepared for them when the opportunity presented itself. What actions can you take to be prepared next time?

What are the things you have accomplished that would be deemed as high risk or that few people would have the courage to do them?

What is your risk appetite? Do you limit your endeavours because you are scared of taking risks?

Are there fears in your own life that you have not yet dealt with? Things that are paralysing you, preventing you from moving forward? Frequently these fears are deep-rooted and irrational, so you may take longer to work through this than any of the others. That is okay.

I challenge you to identify at least one action that you can take to overcome the fear. It may be just one step, but embark on the journey and see where it takes you.

Given you are reading this book, you will be able to grasp where it has taken me.

THE INFINITE LIST
WRAP UP

Reflecting on what you have accomplished in your life can be challenging, particularly if there is no finite list against which to measure your experiences. Do not underestimate the amazing things you have done just because you had not considered them noteworthy or no one else considered them to be important or significant.

Choosing what to do is trickier when there is no predefined list to select from. When the list of possibilities is infinite, it requires you to dig deep, to think more about your own life rather than what others have done or written on their *bucket list*. It entails thinking about your own passions, and what is important to you.

Keep dreaming and looking for opportunities! You never know when you may be presented with a chance to do something. Be ready to seize the opportunity.

Do not be limited by what others are doing or even by your own ideas. You may be surprised by what you find.

RE-CALIBRATING YOUR COMPASS

Are there incredible things that you have accomplished
or experienced in your life? Why do you consider them
incredible? How do they contribute to your passion?

Do you feel as though you have missed opportunities?
Why? How can you position yourself to take advantage of
opportunities that present themselves in the future?

What other experiences have you had that others
are interested in but have not done?

How can you help? Identify the actions you can
take to inspire people to action and do them!

Have you done or achieved things and cannot understand
why others do not share the desire? Does it matter?

Do you have unrealised dreams? Things you have been wishing
you could do or had done? Which of these unrealised dreams
are you going to tackle? Are there some best kept as dreams?
For those that are to be tackled what are you going to do
and when? How can you ensure that you keep dreaming?

Even the list of questions is infinite. Take some time to ponder
what other questions you could be asking yourself and work
through the answers. I would love to hear what they are.

10

Looking Forward

I hope that my stories have prompted you to think back on your life—not to have regrets, but to celebrate the journey, understand all the things that have brought you to where you are and provide a springboard into where you are going.

DVT/PE presented me with an unexpected opportunity to look back on my life. Something that happened to me that was not of my making and certainly would not have been of my choosing changed the trajectory of my life. And whilst not always easy, the change has been largely positive.

Reflecting on my life has afforded me the chance to take stock of the wide array of things that I have undertaken. I am so grateful to have been able to appreciate all the amazing things that I have done and achieved, the wonderful people I have met along the way, and to acknowledge the many blessings. To give myself kudos for what I have done. It has been so encouraging and confidence-building to take the time to *celebrate success.*

With the benefit of hindsight, I have become increasingly aware that my high level of motivation had driven me to do so many things, to live a full life now rather than plan one for the future. I began to realise how much I have experienced and accomplished. I have undertaken many of the endeavours that others set their sights on doing and often never do. In many instances, this has been totally inadvertent. I can honestly say that I have never made a *bucket list*, have never considered making one. And, I am glad I didn't. If I had written a *bucket list*, I may have been so focused on the list, on the planning, that I would have missed out on the doing. A bit like the item on the to-do list or the new year's resolution that never makes its way to the diary to be completed. I have little doubt my life would have been a lot less rewarding had I spent my time focusing on making lists. I am so happy that I used my energy *to do rather than plan.*

Having completed so many things, I realise now that if I had made a list, it could have limited me and continue to do so. I may even be tempted to slow down in case I run out of stuff to do. After all, if I were to use the "Top 20" list as a reference, I only have a handful of items still to do before I die. As my mother says "the day we stop learning, growing and trying something new is the day we die", and I am by no means ready to do that yet. This means I need to ensure that I keep *looking for inspiration—and keep dreaming.*

Arguably the greatest outcome of reflecting on the past was my recognizing that it is not about trying to achieve someone else's list of goals. It is certainly not about competing with others to do what they consider noteworthy activities, adventures or achievements. At some point, I realised that so much of what I had chosen to do was as a result of comparing myself with others or to meet or exceed what I considered the expectations of other people. As the baby sister, I competed to get attention. As the youngest in my class at school, I felt the need to be the best at everything to avoid being bullied. I kept on having to do everything that everyone else did—and better. Even though some of the things I had been through may have given me what Carter would have described as joy, many of them made little or no contribution to what is important to me. That does not mean I should not have done them or that they were a waste of time, but I began to recognise a need to consider how that impacted what I would focus on going forward. How I would focus on things that brought *value to my life and to the people around me.*

Before moving forward, it was important for me to make peace with the present and to acknowledge what had happened in the past. To identify the areas where I had gaps, felt as though I had failed or had not done things I had wanted to. To understand how what I had been through in my life had all contributed to my being the person that I am. Even to accept that, fit as I was, I was not getting any younger. I had to come to terms with my own fallibility. Then I could decide on what I was going to do based on what excited me, what I deemed of value to myself and to others.

That does not mean that the reflection is over, that now I have it all together and have started living the perfect life. It by no means implies that I have not continued to stall, be paralysed by fear or worry about things left undone. But it has propelled me to seek to make intentional choices, to spend time with people, to fight any desire to procrastinate and to strive to live a life of no regrets. I do not want to spend too much time doing things that are of lesser value at the expense of those that would bring me or others joy. I do not want to sacrifice what gives me and others joy for momentary pleasure or kudos from others.

I strongly encourage you not to wait until a health crisis or other dramatic event hits. Celebrate what you have, the things you have done and achieved. Take courage from where you have done things that were beyond your imagination. Learn from those times when you have tried but not fully succeeded. Take on board the wisdom gained from those endeavours that you deem to be total disasters. Identify what it is that you're truly passionate about.

If you have been pondering the points at the end of each chapter, you likely have everything you need to move forward. If not, you may like to start by crossing out all or some of the "Top 20" items. For those that you have done, celebrate them. If they are not at all relevant to your abilities, dreams, aspirations or desires, then ditch them.

1. ~~See the Northern Lights~~
2. ~~Run A Marathon = numerous, including Paris for my 25th wedding anniversary~~
3. ~~Take An African Safari = every year as a child, Ngorongoro and Serengeti~~
4. ~~Write A Story~~
5. ~~Walk The Great Wall of China~~
6. ~~Learn to Play an Instrument~~
7. ~~Snorkel the Barrier Reef~~
8. ~~Sky-Dive~~
9. ~~Own A Dog~~
10. ~~See The Pyramids of Giza~~
11. ~~Learn Another Language~~
12. ~~Ride a Gondola in Venice~~
13. ~~Drive Across the Country~~
14. ~~View Paris from the Eiffel Tower~~
15. ~~Hike the Pacific Crest Trail~~
16. ~~Take an Alaskan Cruise~~
17. ~~See Your Favorite Band~~
18. ~~Go Glamping (is this real?)~~
19. ~~Visit Stonehenge~~
20. ~~Climb Kilimanjaro~~

Alternatively, if you have already formulated your own list of "things to do before you kick the bucket", you may wish to follow the same process. Revel in those that you have done, get rid of those that are not of value to the life you wish to lead, and do those that you do believe will give you and others joy. Start celebrating the other amazing things you have done or experienced that have never been featured on a list. This could include things like people you have met, places you have been, and things you have achieved.

Come to terms with where you are now, your current situation. This may include limitations such as health issues, insufficient funds, or responsibilities such as young children. On the other side of the spectrum, it may be that you are experiencing newfound freedom, that your children have just left home or you have just won the lottery.

Ask yourself whether you are more of a Carter or an Edward from the movie. Like Edward, do you value the exciting, glamorous things that will impress or are you more like Carter, simply looking for the things that bring you joy? For a time, Carter went looking for exciting things, things that his new friend thought were important, but he soon came to the realisation that those were not what brought him joy. Ultimately, Carter abandoned the idea of ticking items off the list to return to the simplicity of his life, his family, and his faith. To what he deemed brought him joy. He realised they were his source of true happiness. He no longer wanted to sacrifice what gave him joy for the pursuit of someone else's fantasies.

On the other hand, Edward dies climbing up a mountain. After his death, the words of the narrator highlight the marked difference between the two men. "Even now I cannot understand the measure of a life, but I can tell you this. I know that when he died, his eyes were closed and his heart was open. And I'm pretty sure he was happy with his final resting place because he was buried on the mountain. And that was against the law."

Different choices but neither one right nor wrong. Both made the conscious choice to finish their lives in line with their own values and priorities.

In the movie, Carter makes a profound statement. He says "You measure yourself by the people who measure themselves by you." It is not only about our own joy, but about the joy we give to others. Rather than follow someone else's list—maybe you can be the thought leader. Perhaps you can or do inspire others to dream and embark on things they had never have thought about. Or possibly you are able to motivate others to push forward when they feel unable to start or to keep going. In addition to achieving your own dreams you can contribute to the lives of others.

Having looked back on your life and come to terms with your current circumstances and what motivates you, you have all the elements to shoot ahead with vigour. The *bucket list* may be deemed to be a life-planning tool. Based on my reflections, and somewhat controversially, I would describe it as potentially a "life-hindering" tool. Whilst I have found the "Top 20" to be a good starting point for celebrating what I have accomplished, if I had managed my life by a *bucket list*, I would have missed out on doing so much. I am so glad that I have kept dreaming and putting myself out there to take advantage of opportunities.

Get doing instead of planning. Stop worrying about the things you have not done. Yes, I am challenging you to be ruthless. Do not put your energy into listing what you will do before you kick the bucket. If you do, life will pass you by, and you will likely not make the most of the life you have left.

Get rid of the *bucket list* and live your life. Ultimately you will end up with a list. Rather than consisting of the things you think you **should** do, it will be a list of what you **have** done. It will be formed from the bottom up. It will be your own, unique list. What you have done and not what you would like to do someday—and definitely not a list of what others would like to do or think you should do. The good thing is that you will always have achieved it!

For me, I take encouragement from a verse in the Bible. The writer of Ecclesiastes said, 'We should make the most of what God gives, both the bounty and the capacity to enjoy it, accepting what's given and delighting in the work. It's God's gift! God deals out joy in the present, the now" (Ecclesiastes 5:19 MSG).

Learn to enjoy this wonderful gift of life in the present.

Gratitude

I am truly grateful to every person in my life
who has contributed to my life story.

The book would not have existed without the experiences that make up the stories. I could not have accomplished any of these things without all of those that have inspired me.

I thank God, who has granted me countless blessings and abilities to accomplish things beyond my wildest dreams. I hope that I have used the gifts and talents that you have given me wisely.

I thank my parents for encouraging me to dream and for giving me the opportunities to realise many of them. I am forever grateful to my mother, for instilling in me a zest for life and for always being eager to hear about my adventures.

To my husband, best friend and greatest supporter, Walter, thank you for entertaining my ideas, and for being prepared to get out there with me on so many of my exploits—they have been much more fun with you by my side.

Thank you to all the friends, agents, and guides who have helped me plan and execute many of my pursuits.

Christopher Hitchens, an American journalist, is quoted as saying, "Everyone has a book inside them." Although he also added "which is exactly where it should, I think, in most cases, remain," I am glad to have had the chance to get mine out. A big THANK YOU to those who have made this book possible.

I could not have arrived at this stage without the many who have encouraged me to put my experiences on paper and release them to the world, the many who have been instrumental in the successful completion of this book. It would be impossible to list all names and it is difficult to find adequate words to convey how much I owe these people.

Once again, to my husband, Walter, thank you for being my greatest fan, walking every step of this journey with me, and always believing in me. For standing by me through the blood, sweat, and tears.

To Jeanne, publisher extraordinaire, thank you for sharing your extensive experience and guiding me through the labyrinth of words, providing insights to help my polishing efforts. Without your expert guidance, this book would not have materialised. Thanks for believing in what I had to share from the first time you read my manuscript.

To Andrew, author and book coach, thank you for reaching out at the right time to trigger the book-writing process. For your enthusiasm and for constantly reminding me that I can do it.

To those who gave your valuable time to read the early edition of the book, I am grateful for your support and honest feedback.

I am grateful:

To my fellow authors who have provided me with encouragement and tips at various stages along the writing journey.

To the many friends who have supported and prayed for me. To those who have encouraged me to write a book, believing that I had interesting tales to tell. To those who believed in me when I didn't.

To the coaching clients, friends, and connections that my stories have inspired in the past. You have helped me keep going during those times when I questioned whether I could have an impact on others.

Last, but certainly not least, I thank you, the reader for making the journey worthwhile. To all those who pick up this book, thank you for giving my words a chance to impact your life. To the ones reading it, may you experience the courage and joy contained in these pages. May you have the audacity to dream and find the courage to pursue those dreams.

About the Author

Born in South Africa, Glenda Mitchell moved to Australia after completing her degree.

A motivational coach, keynote speaker, and published author, Glenda combines her business degree with over 30 years of corporate experience, working with individuals and teams across various industries. She relishes encouraging others to get the most out of themselves. Every decision Glenda makes, and every interaction she engages in, has at its very core the purpose of challenging herself and others to dream and to do things that they may have only fantasised about but didn't imagine that they would ever do.

Glenda describes herself as an adventure-seeking, marathon-running traveller. She has visited more than 60 countries around the globe, choosing as many adventurous pursuits as she can wherever she goes.

In 2016, Glenda survived a significant health scare. Whilst always being a motivated person—sometimes to the point of craziness—it took a health emergency for Glenda to reassess her priorities and arrive at a more balanced view of living her life. Like many on a career track, she had been planning for that time in the future when she could do more of the things she wanted to do. The health scare made her realise that, whilst she was relatively young, healthy and fit, she wasn't invincible.

Within a year, she and her husband Walter sold up their home, resigned from full-time corporate work, and started what many would call "living the dream." Turning a health scare into purposeful action, she transformed motivation into action and calls on others to do the same. She hopes that this book will trigger others to reflect on their own lives, celebrate their achievements, and—if necessary—create their own pivotal moment before it is done for them.

In *Kicking out The Bucket List*, Glenda shares some of her drive to excel. She tells the stories of the adventures and experiences she has embarked on before and after 2016. Those stories that have inspired coaching clients, friends and strangers, to want to do the activity themselves. Through her book, Glenda encourages others to celebrate the things they have achieved. She urges them to focus on "doing" rather than "wishing." On doing *their* things, not the things that *others* are passionate about. To make intentional decisions that result in making the most out of the gifts that they have been given. To live every moment of the day, making the most of the time and talents we have been given!

Staying Connected

Glenda would love to hear from you!
If this book has driven you to do something new or something you've wanted to do, Glenda would love to hear your story.

Glenda would love to work with you in a coaching relationship in person or online!
If you need help working through the questions posed in this book or implementing the changes, consider engaging Glenda as your coach. She can work with you on the practical things that you can do—using her 7Ps approach to *Living Life with Intention and Passion*.

If you need help planning or executing your next endeavour, adventure or experience, contact Glenda.

Glenda would love to work with your group in person or online!
If you need someone to energise your audience or motivate your team, consider engaging Glenda as a speaker or facilitator. Her most popular keynotes are:

Life is Like a Marathon
The 7Ps: Living Life with Intention and Passion

Contact Details

Website: https://mitchell.news/

LinkedIn: https://www.linkedin.com/in/glendamitchell11/

Email: kickingoutthebucketlist@mitchell.news

www.ingramcontent.com/pod-product-compliance
Lightning Source LLC
Chambersburg PA
CBHW071403120626
46546CB00002B/793